CAMBRIDGE NATIONAL LEVEL 1/LEV

Enterprise and Marketing

Revision Guide and Workbook

Laura Chambers & Julie Whatford

CAMBRIDGE
UNIVERSITY PRESS

University Printing House, Cambridge CB2 8BS, United Kingdom

One Liberty Plaza, 20th Floor, New York, NY 10006, USA

477 Williamstown Road, Port Melbourne, VIC 3207, Australia

314–321, 3rd Floor, Plot 3, Splendor Forum, Jasola District Centre, New Delhi – 110025, India

103 Penang Road, #05–06/07, Visioncrest Commercial, Singapore 23846

Cambridge University Press is part of the University of Cambridge.

It furthers the University's mission by disseminating knowledge in the pursuit of education, learning and research at the highest international levels of excellence.

www.cambridge.org
Information on this title: www.cambridge.org/9781009106498

© Cambridge University Press & Assessment 2022

First published 2022

20 19 18 17 16 15 14 13 12 11 10 9 8 7 6 5 4 3 2 1

Printed in Poland by Opolgraf

A catalogue record for this publication is available from the British Library

ISBN 978-1-009-10649-8 Revision Guide and Workbook with Digital Access (2 Years)
ISBN 978-1-009-10283-4 Digital Revision Guide and Workbook (2 Years)
ISBN 978-1-009-10284-1 Digital Revision Guide and Workbook (1 Year Site Licence)

Additional resources for this publication at www.cambridge.org/9781009106498

Cambridge University Press has no responsibility for the persistence or accuracy of URLs for external or third-party internet websites referred to in this publication, and does not guarantee that any content on such websites is, or will remain, accurate or appropriate. Information regarding prices, travel timetables, and other factual information given in this work is correct at the time of first printing but Cambridge University Press does not guarantee the accuracy of such information thereafter.

Thanks to Getty Images for permission to reproduce images: *Cover* Maskot/Getty Images; *Inside* Korrawin Khanta/EyeEm/Getty Images; Atit Phetmuangtong/EyeEm/Getty Images

....

....

Contents

Preparing for the exam

Unit R067: Enterprise and marketing concepts

Revision Guide

Workbook

Glossary

Answers

Preparing for the exam

Your Revision Guide and Workbook

This Revision Guide will support you in preparing for the exam for Unit R067: Enterprise and marketing concepts. This is the externally assessed unit of your course.

The Revision Guide contains two types of pages as shown below:

- Content pages help you revise the content you need to know.
- Workbook pages with practice exam-style questions to help you prepare for your exam.

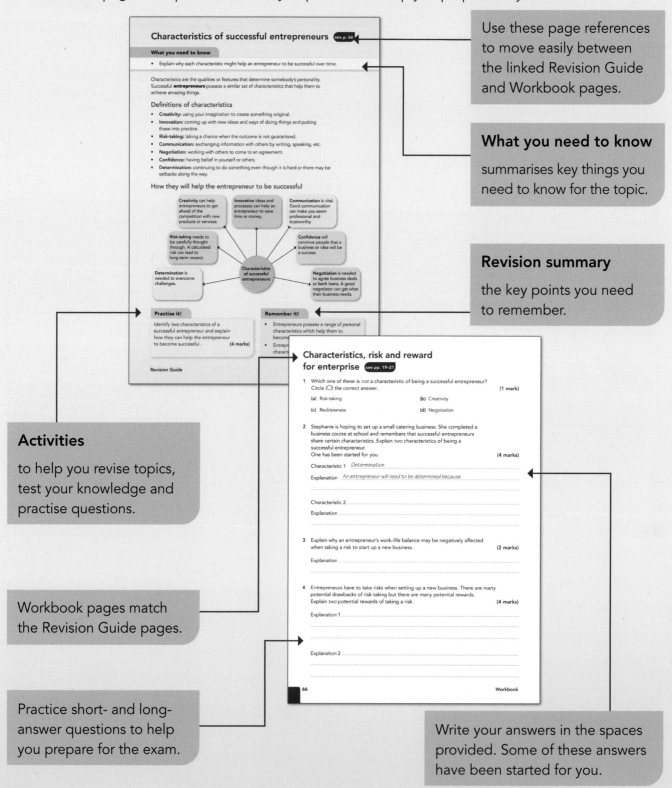

Use these page references to move easily between the linked Revision Guide and Workbook pages.

What you need to know

summarises key things you need to know for the topic.

Revision summary

the key points you need to remember.

Activities

to help you revise topics, test your knowledge and practise questions.

Workbook pages match the Revision Guide pages.

Practice short- and long-answer questions to help you prepare for the exam.

Write your answers in the spaces provided. Some of these answers have been started for you.

Planning your revision

Countdown to the exam

Revision checklists are a good way for you to plan and structure your revision.
They also allow you to make sure you have covered everything you need to cover.

Revision planner checklist

Time before the exam	Things to do	
6–8 weeks	• Draw up a revision timetable so that you know how much time you have to get through everything.	☐
	• Use the revision checklist to work out which topics you need to cover.	☐
	• Use the topic area headings and bullets to organise your notes and to make sure you've covered everything in the specification.	☐
	• Don't do too much in one day – a couple of hours of good-quality work in a day is better than trying to cram.	☐
4–6 weeks	• Work out which of the areas you still find difficult and plan when you'll cover them.	☐
	• You may be able to discuss tricky topics with your teacher or class colleagues.	☐
	• As you feel you've got to grips with some of the knowledge, you can 'tick off' the parts that have been worrying you.	☐
	• Make the most of the revision sessions you're offered in class. Don't skip them!	☐
1 week	• Make a daily plan to revise those few topics you're not happy with and look back at your revision cards (see below) if you've made some.	☐
Day before	• Try not to cram today – get some exercise and relax in the afternoon.	☐
	• Make sure you know what time and where the exam is and put all your things out (pencils, pens, calculator, bus pass, water) ready for the next day.	☐
	• Get a good night's sleep!	☐

Revise it!

Using the example above, create your own revision checklist. Identify areas that you are not so confident about and think of ways to tackle these.

Revision tips

Choose the methods that work for you

For example:

- use highlighters for key words and phrases
- make note cards
- use mnemonics (the first letter of words): for example, the elements of the marketing mix are sometimes referred to as the 4Ps as the first letter of each element is P.

Plan your revision

Make a list of all the key dates from when you start your revision up to the exam date.

Don't cram!

Plan to space your revision out so that you don't do everything at once!

Take breaks

Plan regular breaks in your revision. Go for a short walk or get some fresh air. It will make you more focused when you do revise!

Identify your strengths and weaknesses

Complete the 'Revision checklist' at the end of each chapter and identify areas that you feel less confident about. Allow additional time to revise these areas.

Learn everything!

Questions can be asked about **any area** of the specification.

It is easier to answer a question if you have revised everything.

Stay healthy!

Exercise, fresh air, good food and staying hydrated all help your revision.

Practise!

Practising exam-style questions will help you get to grips with the question types, time pressure and format of the exam.

Attend revision classes!

Don't skip revision classes – it can really help to revise with your friends as well as by yourself.

Use mind maps!

Mind maps are great for connecting ideas and memorising information more easily and quickly.

Preparing for the exam

Revision techniques

Flash cards/revision cards

These are useful for summarising content, key word definitions and important facts. Use colours to make certain things stand out – for example, you could use different colours for advantages and disadvantages or for key words. You can test yourself using the revision cards.

Mind maps

These are a really useful visual summary of information and you can put them on the wall. They allow you to show links between ideas and concepts. You can start by adding the topic to the centre of the diagram and then add the sub-topics around that and a summary of the information.

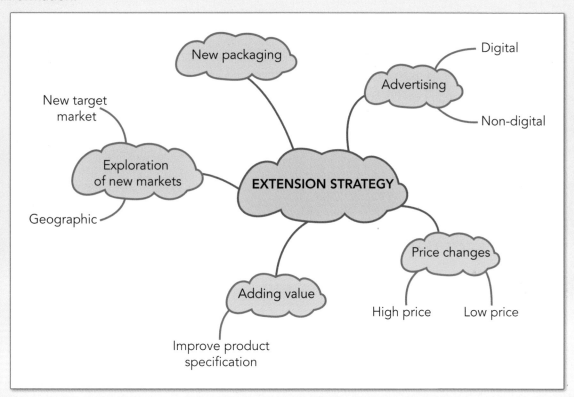

Revise it!

Create a mind map for a topic of your choice.

Highlighting

Making notes and highlighting key areas to go back to is a good way of working out what you know and don't know. You can then use these notes as you come to your final revision. You can use different colours to highlight different factors or different types of information.

For example, there are four different forms of ownership for business start-ups that you need to know for R067. You could highlight:

- key terms in yellow
- ownership in purple
- advantages in green
- disadvantages in orange.

This will help you to instantly identify the key points as part of your revision.

- Sole trader – a business owned by one person. They can make their own decisions and do not have to share profits earned. However, the owner has unlimited liability.
- Partnership – a business owned by two or more partners. They can share skills/experiences to run the business and make decisions. However, profits must be shared and there is a risk of disagreements.
- Limited liability partnerships – a business owned by two or more partners but benefiting from limited liability. However, profits are still shared and disagreements may occur.
- Private Limited Company – a business owned by shareholders with limited liability. Additional capital can be raised by selling more shares with the permission of the other shareholders. Decision making may be slower, though.

Summaries

On the revision pages of this book, you'll find summaries of key ideas and themes. Use these to help you summarise the key points you'll need to remember to answer questions on those topics. For example, you need to know the characteristics of successful entrepreneurs. You can make a summary of these yourself – and if you think through these points in the exam, you are more likely to remember them.

Mnemonics

A **mnemonic** is another useful way of remembering key facts by using the first letter of each of the parts to make up a memorable phrase. For example, the elements of the marketing mix are sometimes referred to as the 4Ps as the first letter of each element is P. This is a good way to remember **P**roduct, **P**lace, **P**rice and **P**romotion.

Quizzes

Many people enjoy quizzes, and creating and sharing quizzes with your friends and class is a great way to remember facts and concepts. You could suggest to your teacher that, in pairs, you create a quiz of ten questions each week and go through them with another pair – swapping answers. It's also a good way for you to check your knowledge. Make a note of the areas where you really didn't know the answer and add these to your revision list.

Practice questions

Doing past papers and practice exam questions is an essential part of your revision. It prepares you for answering different types of exam questions and allows you to become familiar with the wording of the questions used by OCR.

You should also use the mark scheme. This will help you understand how to get full marks for each question.

It is helpful to highlight key words in exam questions so you're clear what the question is asking before you answer it.

Preparing for the exam

Getting ready for the exam

Use the revision checklist and all your revision material to make sure you are as prepared as possible; practise plenty of exam questions and quick quizzes.

In the exam

Give yourself time to complete the whole paper, and check through it for mistakes. Most importantly, try to stay calm and relaxed – remember, this is your time to show off what you know!

Get plenty of sleep

Make sure you get a good night's sleep the night before the exam. Don't stay up late cramming as you need time to switch off and relax before going to bed.

Keep hydrated but don't drink too much

It's important that you stay hydrated but don't overdo it or you'll be running to the toilet. Exams can make you a bit nervous too which means you might need to go to the toilet a bit more frequently. Water is best.

Eat a good, healthy meal

Have a good, healthy meal that you enjoy the night before the exam and a filling breakfast on the day of the exam to give you a boost ready for your exam.

Getting ready for the exam

Make sure you have all the things you need

Get everything ready the night before – including all writing equipment, a calculator if you need one (and are allowed one), a water bottle, tissues if you have a sniff, and any identification you might need (candidate number if you have been given one).

Set your alarm

If your exam is in the morning, set an alarm or two so you have plenty of time to get to the exam. If you're still worried about oversleeping, ask a friend or someone in your family to make sure you're up.

Arrive in plenty of time

Know when and where the exam is. Get there at least 15 minutes before it starts. If your exam is in an unfamiliar part of the school and away from where you normally study, you might have to leave home a bit earlier. Don't be distracted on the way!

Don't be tempted to do too much cramming

Too much last-minute cramming can scramble your brain! You may find that being relaxed will help you recall the facts you need rather than attempting last-minute cramming, but you may also want to revise the key facts before setting off for the exam.

What to expect in the exam

As part of your qualification in Enterprise and Marketing you will be taking an exam that is worth 40 percent of your marks. So it's important that from the beginning you start to think about the exam and the skills you'll need to get the best possible grade. Answering exam questions is a skill. Like any other skill, it can be learnt, practised and improved.

Below is an outline of what to expect in the exam, the types of questions and what the paper looks like. You need to answer **all** the questions.

Types of questions to expect in the exam

Exam questions can be asked about any area of the specification, which means that you have to learn everything!

The exam paper will contain four types of question.

Question type	Description
Multiple-choice question (MCQ)	• A question with four answer options. • Worth 1 mark.
Short-answer question	• Usually requires a one-word answer or a simple sentence. • Worth between 1 and 3 marks, depending upon how many answers you have to state or identify.
Medium-answer question	• Usually requires a longer answer to show your knowledge and understanding of the topic. • Worth between 3 and 6 marks.
Long-answer question	• Open-response question where you are expected to do a piece of extended writing which could ask you to analyse the advantages/disadvantages of a topic or alternatively consider two courses of action that an entrepreneur needs to choose between. You will consider the benefits and limitations of each course of action in light of the business scenario/context and then justify a decision. • Worth 6 or 8 marks. • These questions allow you to be assessed on the quality of your written communication.

Understanding the language of the exam

The command word is the key term that tells you how to answer the question. It is essential to know what the different command words mean and what they are asking you to do. It is easy to confuse the words and provide too much information, not enough information or the wrong information. The tables below will help you understand what each command word is asking you to do.

Command words that ask you to get creative

Command word	OCR definition	How you should approach it
Create	• Produce a visual solution to a problem (for example, a mind map, flow chart or visualisation).	Show your answer in a visual way. You might want to use a mind map, flow chart or a diagram. Think about what is the best way to show the required information.
Draw	• Produce a picture or diagram.	Create a picture/diagram to show the relevant information.

Command words that ask you to choose the correct answer

Command word	OCR definition	How you should approach it
Choose	• Select an answer from options given.	Pick the option that you think is correct.
Circle	• Select an answer from options given.	Draw a circle around the right answer.
Identify	• Select an answer from options given. • Recognise, name or provide factors or features.	Either choose the correct answer from those given, or write the name, factors or features that are asked for.

Command words that ask you to add to something

Command word	OCR definition	How you should approach it
Annotate	• Add information, for example, to a table, diagram or graph, until it is final. • Add all the needed or appropriate parts.	Add short notes to the table/diagram/graph to say what each part is.
Complete	• Add all the needed or appropriate parts. • Add information, for example, to a table, diagram or graph, until it is final.	Add the information that is missing. Often you will need to give just one word as an answer, but sometimes you may need to write more. You may need to finish drawing a diagram or graph.
Fill in	• Add all the needed or appropriate parts. • Add information, for example, to a table, diagram or graph, until it is final.	Add the information that is missing. Often you will need to give just one word as an answer but sometimes you may need to write more.
Label	• Add information, for example, to a table, diagram or graph, until it is final. • Add all the needed or appropriate parts.	This often refers to a diagram or a picture. Add words or short phrases to say what each part is. You could add arrows next to your label that point to the right part of the diagram/graph.

Command words that ask you to do your maths

Command word	OCR definition	How you should approach it
Calculate	• Get a numerical answer showing how it has been worked out.	Do your maths. Give the final answer, but make sure you show how you got there.

Command words that ask you to give the main points

Command word	OCR definition	How you should approach it
Outline	• Give a short account, summary or description.	Write about the main points. Don't write lots of detailed information.
State	• Give factors or features. • Give short, factual answers.	Give a short answer that names factors or features of something. Sometimes you will be asked to give a certain number of factors/features.

Command words that ask you to be factual

Command word	OCR definition	How you should approach it
Describe	• Give an account including all the relevant characteristics, qualities or events. • Give a detailed account of.	This is the 'what'. Write about **what** something is.
Explain	• Give reasons for and/or causes of. • Use the words 'because' or 'therefore' in answers.	This is the 'how' and the 'why'. Write about **how** something happens or works and **why** it does.

Command words that ask you to give an opinion

Command word	OCR definition	How you should approach it
Analyse	• Separate or break down information into parts and identify its characteristics or elements. • Explain the pros and cons of a topic or argument and make reasoned comments. • Explain the impacts of actions using a logical chain of reasoning.	This term wants you to write about the details. Write about each part in turn, giving key information and saying what is good or bad about it.
Compare and contrast	• Give an account of the similarities and differences between two or more items or situations.	'Compare' means to say what is the **same** about two (or more) things. 'Contrast' means to say what is **different** about two (or more) things.
Discuss	• Present, analyse and evaluate relevant points (for example, for/against an argument).	Write about something in detail, including its strengths and weaknesses. Say what you think about each side of the argument. You don't need to take a side.
Evaluate	• Make a reasoned qualitative judgement considering different factors and using available knowledge/experience.	Write down the arguments for and against something. Then give your opinion about which is the stronger argument.
Justify	• Give good reasons for offering an opinion or reaching a conclusion.	Write what you think would be the best option and say why you think this. Give evidence to support your answer.

> **Practise it!**
>
> Now go to www.cambridge.org/go and complete the practice questions on understanding the exam command words.

Common exam mistakes

Common mistakes	Why it matters!	Solutions
Not attempting a question	You won't get any marks for a blank answer.	• Answer every question. • Write something – you may pick up a few marks, which can add up to make the difference between grades. • Use your general knowledge. • State the obvious. • Think 'What would my teacher say to that?'
Not answering the question that is asked	You won't get any marks for writing about another topic or for responding to the wrong command word.	• Know what the command words are looking for. • RTQ – read the question. • ATQ – answer the question.
Not providing enough points to achieve the marks	You won't gain full marks if you haven't expanded on your answer.	• Look at the number of marks next to the question – 1 mark = 1 point; 2 marks = 2 points, 3 marks = 3 points, etc. • Consider if the question requires further explanation or discussion.

Answering long-answer questions

Planning your answer

To help you organise your thoughts, it is helpful to plan your answer for 8-mark questions. You don't need to take too long. A spider diagram, for example, will help you get your answer in the right order and it makes sure you don't forget anything. For example:

Revise it!

Create a spider diagram plan like the one above for the following question:

'Idara is preparing to set up a new business and wants to carry out market research to understand customers' needs/wants.

Explain *two* primary market research methods that Idara could use.'   **(8 marks)**

Tip: You could refer to pages 23–24 of the Revision Guide to help you.

The exam paper

Make sure you know how long you have got.

OCR
Oxford Cambridge and RSA

<<Date>> – <<Morning/Afternoon>>

OCR Level 1/Level 2 Cambridge Nationals in Enterprise and Marketing

R067/01 Enterprise and marketing concepts

Sample Assessment Material (SAM)

Time allowed: 1 hour 15 minutes

You can use:
• A calculator

Write clearly in black ink. **Do not write in the barcodes.**

Centre number | | | | | | Candidate number | | | | |

First name(s) _____

Last name _____

INSTRUCTIONS
• Use black ink.
• Write your answer to each question in the space provided.
• Write your answer to each question in the space provided. If students require additional answer space, lined paper may be available at the end of the answer booklet in a live question paper. Remember the question number(s) must be clearly shown.
• Answer **all** the questions.

INFORMATION
• The total mark for this paper is **70**.
• The marks for each question are shown in brackets **[ ]**.
• This document has **16** pages.

ADVICE
• Read each question carefully before you start your answer.

Write your first name and surname clearly in the box.

Ensure that you write clear, structured answers so that you can get maximum marks.

6

Section B

Answer the questions in Section B using the information in the scenario below.

You have just finished a photography qualification and live near a number of famous tourist attractions which you enjoy photographing. During the final months of your qualification, you started selling framed copies of your photos through an online marketplace. Using specialist software, you give your photos a hand-painted effect. You use a local supplier who then prints and frames the pictures ready for you to sell.

Demand for your pictures is growing from people who visit the area. You have set up as a sole trader business to sell your pictures.

11 (a) Other than operating as a sole trader, identify two types of business ownership that you could have considered.

1 ....

2 ....

[2]

(b) Analyse **two** disadvantages of running your photography business as a sole trader.

Disadvantage 1 ....

....

....

....

....

....

....

....

Disadvantage 2 ....

....

....

....

....

....

....

....

[6]

Revision checklist

Topic area	What you should know			
Topic Area 1: Characteristics, risk and reward for enterprise	**1.1 Characteristics of successful entrepreneurs**			
	• Characteristics of successful entrepreneurs	☐	☐	☐
	1.2 Potential rewards for risk-taking and potential drawbacks for risk-taking			
	• Potential rewards for risk-taking	☐	☐	☐
	• Potential drawbacks for risk-taking	☐	☐	☐
Topic Area 2: Market research to target a specific customer	**2.1 The purpose of market research**			
	• The purpose of market research	☐	☐	☐
	2.2 Primary market research methods			
	• Primary market research methods 1	☐	☐	☐
	• Primary market research methods 2	☐	☐	☐
	2.3 Secondary market research sources			
	• Secondary market research sources	☐	☐	☐
	• Primary versus secondary market research	☐	☐	☐
	2.4 Types of data			
	• Quantitative and qualitative data	☐	☐	☐
	2.5 Types of market segmentation			
	• Market segmentation	☐	☐	☐
	2.6 The benefits of market segmentation to a business			
	• Benefits of market segmentation	☐	☐	☐
Topic Area 3: What makes a product financially viable	**3.1 Cost of producing the product**			
	• Fixed costs	☐	☐	☐
	• Variable costs	☐	☐	☐
	• Total costs	☐	☐	☐
	3.2 Revenue generated by sales of the product			
	• Revenue generated by sales	☐	☐	☐
	3.3 Profit/loss			
	• Profit and loss 1	☐	☐	☐

	• Profit and loss 2	☐	☐	☐
	3.4 How to use the formula for break-even as an aid to decision making			
	• Break-even	☐	☐	☐
	• Interpreting a break-even graph	☐	☐	☐
	3.5 Importance of cash			
	• The importance of cash	☐	☐	☐
Topic Area 4: Creating a marketing mix to support a product	**4.1, 4.2 The marketing mix elements for a good/service and how the elements of the marketing mix work together**			
	• The marketing mix	☐	☐	☐
	4.3 Types of advertising medium used to attract and retain customers and the appropriateness of each			
	• Non-digital advertising mediums 1	☐	☐	☐
	• Non-digital advertising mediums 2	☐	☐	☐
	• Non-digital advertising mediums 3	☐	☐	☐
	• Digital advertising mediums 1	☐	☐	☐
	• Digital advertising mediums 2	☐	☐	☐
	• Digital advertising mediums 3	☐	☐	☐
	4.4 Sales promotion techniques used to attract and retain customers and the appropriateness of each			
	• Sales promotion techniques 1	☐	☐	☐
	• Sales promotion techniques 2	☐	☐	☐
	• Sales promotion techniques 3	☐	☐	☐
	4.5 Public relations			
	• Public relations (PR)	☐	☐	☐
	4.6 How to sell the good/service to the consumer			
	• How to sell goods and services	☐	☐	☐
	4.7 The product lifecycle			
	• The product lifecycle 1	☐	☐	☐
	• The product lifecycle 2	☐	☐	☐

4.8 Extension strategies for products in the product lifecycle and the appropriateness of each			
• Extension strategies 1	☐	☐	☐
• Extension strategies 2	☐	☐	☐
4.9 Factors to consider when pricing a product to attract and retain customers			
• Factors to consider when pricing a product	☐	☐	☐
4.10 Types of pricing strategies and the appropriateness of each			
• Pricing strategies	☐	☐	☐

Topic Area 5:

Factors to consider when starting up and running an enterprise

5.1 Appropriate forms of ownership for business start-ups			
• Forms of business ownership 1	☐	☐	☐
• Forms of business ownership 2	☐	☐	☐
• Forms of business ownership 3	☐	☐	☐
• Forms of business ownership 4	☐	☐	☐
• Liability	☐	☐	☐
5.2 Source(s) of capital for business start-ups and expansion			
• Sources of capital 1	☐	☐	☐
• Sources of capital 2	☐	☐	☐
5.3 Support for enterprise			
• Support for enterprise	☐	☐	☐

Characteristics of successful entrepreneurs see p. 66

What you need to know

- Explain why each characteristic might help an entrepreneur to be successful over time.

Characteristics are the qualities or features that determine somebody's personality. Successful **entrepreneurs** possess a similar set of characteristics that help them to achieve amazing things.

Definitions of characteristics

- **Creativity:** using your imagination to create something original.
- **Innovation:** coming up with new ideas and ways of doing things and putting these into practice.
- **Risk-taking:** taking a chance when the outcome is not guaranteed.
- **Communication:** exchanging information with others by writing, speaking, etc.
- **Negotiation:** working with others to come to an agreement.
- **Confidence:** having belief in yourself or others.
- **Determination:** continuing to do something even though it is hard or there may be setbacks along the way.

How they will help the entrepreneur to be successful

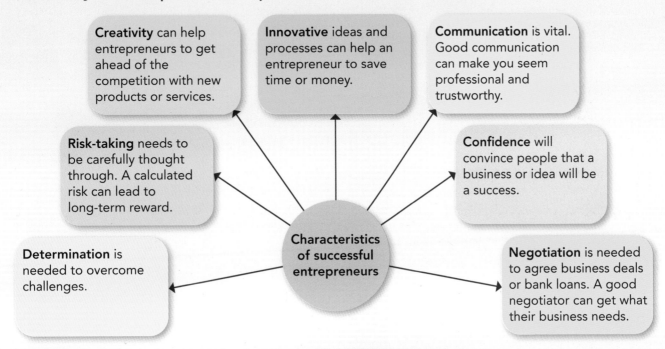

Creativity can help entrepreneurs to get ahead of the competition with new products or services.

Innovative ideas and processes can help an entrepreneur to save time or money.

Communication is vital. Good communication can make you seem professional and trustworthy.

Risk-taking needs to be carefully thought through. A calculated risk can lead to long-term reward.

Confidence will convince people that a business or idea will be a success.

Determination is needed to overcome challenges.

Characteristics of successful entrepreneurs

Negotiation is needed to agree business deals or bank loans. A good negotiator can get what their business needs.

Practise it!

Identify *two* characteristics of a successful entrepreneur and explain how they can help the entrepreneur to become successful. **(4 marks)**

Remember it!

- Entrepreneurs possess a range of personal characteristics which help them to become successful.
- Entrepreneurs will possess these characteristics in different quantities.

Potential rewards for risk-taking see p. 66

What you need to know

- Identify the rewards an entrepreneur may gain for taking risks.

When an entrepreneur starts a business they are taking a risk. There are potentially large rewards for those who are willing to take these risks.

Rewards of risk-taking

Risk-taking is necessary when starting a business, but the rewards can be high.

Financial	• Entrepreneurs will aim to make sure all costs incurred by the business are paid. This is called breaking even. After that, they will aim to make a profit. This can be used to reinvest in the business to develop it further or for the entrepreneur to live off.
Independence	• Many entrepreneurs want to be their own boss. By taking the risk of starting a business, an entrepreneur can decide their own work schedule and make their own decisions.
Self-satisfaction	• Creating a successful business is a proud moment for an entrepreneur. Seeing their first sales or making a profit can lead to a sense of self-satisfaction.
Making a difference/ change	• Some entrepreneurs create their business to help change something. This could be a social/environmental change or something that helps other people. • By identifying a gap in the market, they could improve something that has impacted other people or they could improve someone's life. • Another difference they could make is to provide a product that is not offered by other businesses.

Practise it!

1   State *three* rewards for risk-taking.   **(3 marks)**
2   Explain *one* reward of taking a risk as an entrepreneur.   **(2 marks)**

Remember it!

- Risk-taking has both benefits and drawbacks which must be considered alongside each other.
- By taking the risk of setting up a new business the entrepreneur may enjoy specific rewards.

Potential drawbacks for risk-taking see p. 66

see p. 66

What you need to know

- Identify the potential drawbacks to an entrepreneur of risk-taking.

When an entrepreneur starts a business they must consider the drawbacks of the risk that they may take.

Drawbacks of risk-taking

Starting a business is also a risky thing to do – many businesses fail within the first few years.

Financial	• Not all businesses are **financially viable** – they might run out of money or not make a profit. Despite planning, hard work and market research, some business ideas fail. An entrepreneur may lose the money they used to set up the business and/or find themselves in debt.
Health/ well-being	• Setting up a new business requires hard work and long hours. This may cause stress, especially if the entrepreneur works alone and cannot discuss problems or decisions with others. If they work alone they will have to work if they are unwell, as there is nobody else to cover for them.
Work–life balance	• An entrepreneur may work long hours, especially at the start, leaving little time for relaxation. • Entrepreneurs may have a poor work–life balance, with work taking up all of their time.
Personal relationships	• An entrepreneur may have little time to spend with their children, family and friends, who may become resentful. They may lose touch with family and friends.

Practise it!

1   State *two* drawbacks, other than work–life balance, that come from taking risks.   **(2 marks)**

2   Explain *one* way that a poor work–life balance may affect the entrepreneur.   **(2 marks)**

Remember it!

- Benefits and drawbacks are not only financial.
- Many potential drawbacks can relate to the entrepreneur's health/well-being or relationship with others.

The purpose of market research see p. 67

What you need to know

- Identify and explain the purpose of carrying out market research.

Market research is the process of finding out about the market in which a business operates by collecting, presenting and analysing information and **data**.

To reduce risk	• It helps an entrepreneur to make an informed decision as starting a new business can be very risky. • It also reduces the likelihood of making an incorrect decision.
To aid decision making	• Using market research data helps an entrepreneur to make good, informed decisions that are more likely to lead to a successful result.
To understand the market	• It allows the entrepreneur to know what is happening in the current market and identify any gaps within it. • The entrepreneur can adapt their product to meet changing customer needs and wants.
To gain customers' views and understand their needs and wants	• It helps an entrepreneur to understand their **target market** and the **customer profile** within the target market. • It helps them develop a product that suits the needs of their target market, and allows them to know how and where to promote the product.
To inform product development	• It helps them understand what the target market thinks of the product and what might need changing to make it more desirable before spending money developing the product.
To understand how a good/service complements others on the market	• It allows an entrepreneur to know what others are doing and make informed decisions about features of the product, prices etc. to make their product more appealing and develop a **unique selling point (USP)**.

Practise it!

1 Explain *one* purpose of carrying out market research. **(2 marks)**

2 Explain how market research can inform product development. **(2 marks)**

Remember it!

- Market research is an ongoing process.
- It allows an entrepreneur to understand the needs and wants of their target market so that they can make a product that continues to meet those needs.

Primary market research methods 1 see p. 67

- Identify and define each primary market research method.
- Explain the advantages and disadvantages of each primary market research method.

Primary market research collects first-hand data that has not been collected before. Entrepreneurs usually carry out the research themselves so that it is tailored to the needs of their business.

Observations

Watching and recording customers (e.g. watching what they do or how many people there are in a certain area at a certain time).

Advantages	Disadvantages
• Costs very little and is relatively easy to do • Can see what people actually do rather than what they say they do	• Time-consuming to do and to analyse • People change their behaviour when they know they are being watched • Not clear *why* their behaviour is happening

Focus groups

An interview of a small group of chosen people. A **facilitator** prompts the group with questions and asks them to speak freely to give their opinion on a product or topic.

Advantages	Disadvantages
• Allows participants to expand on their answers so that a deeper insight can be gained • Participants can be selected based on key characteristics	• Some participants might be more dominant than others • Due to cost there are usually only a small number of participants, and that can lead to limited data

Consumer trials

The customer is given a sample product to try.

Advantages	Disadvantages
• Feedback is directly relevant as it is based on a real product • It can be very reliable and honest • A trial is cheaper than a full launch so it reduces financial risk	• It can be quite expensive to give away free products • **Competitors** may hear about the product and copy it • Results are only based on a small **sample**

Test marketing

Products might be launched in one region for a short period of time to test customer reaction.

Advantages	Disadvantages
• Reduces the financial risk of a full launch • Feedback is relevant and reliable as it is based on a real product • Can target specific customers and/or areas	• Results can be misleading as they are based on a small sample • Competitors may hear about the product and launch a similar product first

Revise it!

Create a series of flash cards – state the research method on the front with a description. Write the advantages and disadvantages on the back. Choose a card at random and test yourself regularly.

Remember it!

- Primary research is data that has never been collected before.
- There are *seven* primary research methods: observations, questionnaires, surveys, interviews, **focus groups**, consumer trials and test marketing.

Primary market research methods 2 see p. 68

What you need to know

- Identify and define each primary market research method.
- Explain the advantages and disadvantages of each primary market research method.

Questionnaires, surveys and interviews

Questionnaires	<ul><li>A set of questions designed to find out people's opinions.</li><li>Questions are mainly closed questions with some open questions.</li><li>Completed face-to-face, by email or by post.</li><li>A questionnaire can be part of a survey.</li></ul>
Surveys	<ul><li>The process of collecting data based on questionnaire responses.</li><li>The data collected from indivduals is put together or collated.</li><li>The data is analysed to help make key business decisions.</li><li>Carried out in person, online, by telephone or by post.</li></ul>
Interviews	<ul><li>A structured verbal conversation where the interviewer asks the interviewee questions that have been written beforehand.</li><li>The interviewer might probe the interviewee's answers for more detail.</li><li>Carried out in person, online or by telephone.</li></ul>

Advantages and disadvantages

Advantages	Disadvantages
<ul><li>Questions are carefully planned to gather relevant, up-to-date data</li><li>Data can be easy to analyse</li><li>Can be done in a number of ways, e.g. face to face, online or by telephone or email</li><li>Online surveys are cost-effective</li></ul>	<ul><li>People do not always answer honestly or complete the full survey</li><li>Can be expensive and can take a long time to complete</li><li>May take entrepreneurs away from other aspects of the business</li></ul>

Open questions

- Allow people to give opinions or a more detailed response.
- Responses are more difficult to analyse as everyone could give a different answer.
- Open questions collect **qualitative data**.

Example: 'Why do you like this product?'

Closed questions

- Require the respondent to choose from specific answers such as 'yes' or 'no'.
- Responses are easier to analyse as they are **quantitative**.

Example: 'Do you like this packaging?'

Practise it!

1 State *two* methods of primary market research. **(2 marks)**

2 Analyse *one* advantage and *one* disadvantage of a focus group. **(6 marks)**

Remember it!

- A survey has three steps: collecting data, collating the data and analysing the data.
- Questionnaires are used as part of a survey to collect data.

Secondary market research sources see pp. 67–68

What you need to know

- Identify and define secondary market research.
- Explain the advantages and disadvantages of each secondary market research source.

Secondary market research collects data from sources that already exist. The data has already been collected by another researcher and used for a different purpose.

Sources of secondary market research

Method	Advantages	Disadvantages
Internal data Historical information that the business already has (e.g. sales data, accounts)	• Free to access and relevant to the business • The information is private to the business • Looking at the past helps predict what might happen in the future	• Older data can be unreliable/out of date as the market may have changed • There is no new knowledge
Books and newspapers Newspaper articles can help the entrepreneur understand business information and social trends regionally, nationally and internationally	• Access is easy (e.g. online or as physical copies) • Newspapers are published regularly	• Older books and newspapers can be out of date • Some newspapers can be **biased**
Trade magazines Content is relevant to a specific industry. Aimed at professionals within that industry	• Information is specific to an industry and relevant	• Subscriptions can be expensive
Competitors' data Information about the competitors' business that is publicly available (e.g. profit, revenue, prices, special offers and advertising)	• Data is relevant as it is industry specific • Helps with understanding what competitors are doing	• Not all information (e.g. profit levels and sales figures) may be released
Government publications and statistics Published research, polls and surveys carried out by the government (e.g. Office for National Statistics/Census) to find out what is happening in the country and show key trends	• High-quality research which is accurate • Normally free to access and available online	• Might be out of date. • Information might be biased to support the viewpoint of the publisher
Market research reports, e.g. Mintel Professional market researchers carry out research on specific topics	• Accurate and specialist information	• Produced for a specific purpose so might not be suitable • Often expensive to view

Practise it!

1 Identify *three* secondary market research sources. **(3 marks)**

2 Explain *one* disadvantage of using government publications and statistics. **(2 marks)**

Remember it!

Secondary market research sources contain data that has already been collected, so it is usually easier and cheaper to collect than primary market research, but it may be out of date.

Primary versus secondary market research see pp. 67–68

What you need to know

- Analyse the advantages and disadvantages of primary versus secondary market research.

Primary and secondary market research both have advantages and disadvantages. The choice of research will depend on the entrepreneur's market research aims, budget and timescale.

Primary market research
Data that is collected first hand and that hasn't been collected before

Advantages

- Results are tailored to specific needs of the entrepreneur/business
- Information remains within the business and is not shared with competitors
- Information has been collected recently so is up to date

Disadvantages

- Time-consuming to collect and collate data and may take entrepreneurs away from other aspects of their business
- Can be expensive to carry out

Secondary market research
Data from sources that has been collected before

Advantages

- More cost-effective as it can be free or cheap to access
- There is a vast amount of different information available
- Can save time as the data may already be collated and analysed

Disadvantages

- Competitors have access to the same information
- Information may not be specific to the needs of the business, e.g. the research may have been carried out on a different type of product
- Information may be out of date

Practise it!

Which of the following is an advantage of primary market research? Tick (✓) the correct answer. **(1 mark)**

a It takes a long time to complete. ☐

b It is more cost-effective. ☐

c Information is up to date. ☐

d The research was originally created for another purpose. ☐

Remember it!

- There are advantages and disadvantages to both primary and secondary market research.

- An entrepreneur will often choose their research method or source based on the *time* and the *budget* that they have available.

- Primary and secondary market research may be physical or digital.

Quantitative and qualitative data see p. 69

What you need to know

- State the meaning of qualitative data and quantitative data.
- Explain the benefits and limitations of each type of data.

Market research collects two types of data – quantitative and qualitative – depending on the type of questions asked.

Quantitative data

Data measured in numbers and percentages

Gathered by asking **closed** questions, e.g.:
- Is black a suitable colour for this product? Yes/No
- Which of the three colours do you prefer for the product? Red/Green/Blue

Advantages
- Easy to analyse
- Can be presented as graphs/charts

Disadvantages
- Does not give specific opinions
- Does not allow the business/entrepreneur to understand customers' opinions and thoughts

Qualitative data

Consists of people's opinions and points of view

Gathered from **open** questions, e.g.:
- What do you like about this product?
- Why would you buy product A rather than product B?

Advantages
- Provides a detailed insight into customers' views
- Really valuable detailed information for developing a product

Disadvantages
- May have too many different opinions – so overwhelming, especially if they contradict one another
- More costly to collect
- Takes more time to analyse

Practise it!

1 Explain *one* advantage of **qualitative data**. (2 marks)

2 Identify *two* advantages of **quantitative data**. (2 marks)

Remember it!

- **Quantitative** is like *quantity* – e.g. the data will give a specific number of people who answered for each option, i.e. 20 people said 'yes' and 10 people said 'no'.
- **Qualitative** is like *quality* – the data will give opinions/views as the questions are open questions.

Market segmentation see p. 70

What you need to know

- Identify types of market segmentation.
- Explain why businesses segment their market.

Market segmentation is the process of dividing up a market for a specific product into different groups (**segments**).

Age
Customer wants and needs vary according to age, e.g. children's clothing is smaller in size and may have cartoon characters on it

Lifestyle
Hobbies, interests, opinions and habits influence purchases, e.g. supermarkets have increased the range of vegan products due to growth in environmental awareness

Gender
Some products are aimed at one gender; some are aimed at both, e.g. feminine hygiene products are aimed at women only, with packaging in feminine colours

Market segmentation

Location
Customer wants and needs vary from place to place, e.g. restaurants may adapt their menu to cater for local tastes – haggis in Scotland and Welsh Rarebit

Occupation
People working in certain jobs may need specific products, e.g. a carpenter may require a specific type of saw or chisel

Income
Income varies from person to person; it affects the products people buy, e.g. supermarkets offer a range of products from 'value' to 'premium' products to suit all incomes

Practise it!

1   You are setting up a business selling watches. Explain *two* ways that you could segment the market.   **(4 marks)**

2   Dividing a group of customers by hobbies and interests is an example of which type of market segmentation?   **(1 mark)**

Remember it!

- There are six ways that a business can segment/divide a market to target potential customers and/or tailor their products to suit particular needs.

- The six types are: age, gender, occupation, income, location and lifestyle.

Benefits of market segmentation see p. 70

What you need to know

- Explain the benefits of market segmentation for a business.

Market segmentation helps businesses in different ways.

1. Ensure customers' needs are met and matched

- Customers' needs and wants vary.
- By understanding these needs and wants, a business can alter its product to meet them.
- The entrepreneur can create different products for different segments to better meet specific customers' needs.

2. Increase sales and profits

- Customers are more likely to purchase a product that meets their needs.
- This can lead to more sales for the business.
- If the business focuses on a specific target market, it:
  - can save money (reduce costs) by not marketing to customers who may not buy the product
  - could also charge a higher price if the product meets a specific customer need which is not met by competitors.

3. Target the right product at the right customer

- Marketing and promotion are expensive.
- **Promotion** can be more effective if it is targeted at a specific market who are most likely to buy the product.
- This can also lead to increased sales and profit (see point 2).

4. Increase customer retention and loyalty

- Retaining loyal customers is important for all businesses in order to remain competitive.
- Customers will keep coming back to a business if it produces products that they want and that meet their needs.
- By targeting a specific segment, it is easier to understand the segment's needs and keep customers loyal.

5. Increase market share

- A business wants to sell more than its competitors.
- By effectively targeting a specific market segment, a business can increase its sales and have a bigger share of the market compared to its competitors.

Revise it!

Create a writing frame for the following question:
Analyse *two* ways that market segmentation may increase a business's sales and profit. **(6 marks)**

Remember it!

- Segmenting the market can benefit a business not only by meeting customers' needs and keeping customers loyal, but also by increasing sales and profit, and **market share**.
- There are five main benefits to segmenting the market.

Fixed costs `see pp. 71–72`

What you need to know

- Explain what is meant by fixed costs.
- Be able to calculate fixed costs.

Costs are money that a business has to pay out in order to operate.

What are fixed costs?

Fixed costs are costs that do not change no matter how many products (units) the business produces/sells. Examples are:

- **Advertising** – e.g. the cost of print and digital products to promote the product.
- **Insurance** – to protect business premises (shop/factory/office), machinery and vehicles.
- **Salaries** – payments to employees which do not vary according to the number of hours worked or their level of output. Salaries are often paid monthly.
- **Loan interest** – money that is paid to a lender for borrowing money.
- **Rent** – a payment for the use of a factory, shop, office or other premises.
- **Utilities** – payment for services used to operate the business, e.g. gas, electricity, water, internet and phone.

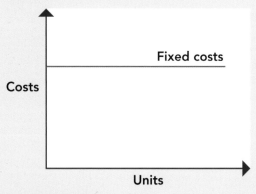

Calculating fixed costs

Total fixed costs are calculated by adding all fixed costs together.

Fixed costs per unit are found by dividing total fixed costs by the number of units produced.

> *Example:*
>
> A business produces 100 units per month and has the following fixed costs per month:
> - rent: £350
> - utilities: £50
> - salaries: £600.
>
> **Total fixed costs** = £350 + £50 + £600
> = £1000
>
> **Fixed costs per unit** = £1000 ÷ 100
> = £10 per unit

Stretch and challenge

Even though fixed costs do **not** change based on **output**, they can change over time. For example:

- Utilities: a gas company might increase or reduce its prices every year, but utilities are essential and still have to be paid for.
- Salaries: employees are often given an annual salary increase.

Practise it!

1   Using an example, explain what is meant by fixed costs.   **(2 marks)**

2   A business has the following costs per month:

advertising: £100   raw materials: £20
salaries: £500   utilities: £50.

Calculate the total fixed costs per year for the business.   **(2 marks)**

Remember it!

- Fixed costs do not change regardless of **output**.
- If a business does not sell any products, it must still pay its fixed costs such as rent and interest on loans.

Variable costs `see pp. 71–72`

see pp. 71–72

What you need to know

- Explain what is meant by variable costs.
- Calculate variable costs.

What are variable costs?

Variable costs are costs that change in line with the **level of output**. The more items that a business produces and sells, the more the variable costs will be. Examples of variable costs are:

- **Raw materials** and **components** – the resources needed to make the product (e.g. a car manufacturer would need the car doors, engine and windscreen to build the car).
- **Packaging** – costs for wrapping the finished product ready for sale/delivery (e.g. a wrapper or box).
- **Wages** – the amount per hour paid to employees. Wages vary according to the number of hours worked (e.g. a waiter might normally work five hours a week and receive £50 but at busier times they might work 30 hours, so they will receive £300 in wages per week).

Calculating variable costs per unit

The formula can be rearranged to find other figures such as the variable cost per unit.

$$\text{Variable cost per unit} = \frac{\text{Variable costs}}{\text{Output}}$$

Example: A business has variable costs of £500 and produces 20 units.

Calculating total variable costs

Total variable costs = variable cost per unit × output

Example:

A business makes 100 units per month and has the following variable costs per month:

- raw materials: £500
- packaging: £50
- wages: £300.

Total variable costs = (£500 + £50 + £300) × 100

= £850 × 100
= £85 000

Variable costs per unit = £500 ÷ 20 = £25

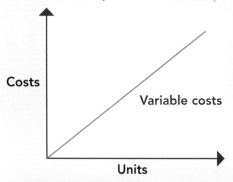

Costs / Variable costs / Units

Practise it!

A business has the following costs:

- utilities: £50
- wages: £150
- salaries: £300
- raw materials: £500
- packaging: £200.

The level of output is 50 units.

Calculate the total variable cost per unit. **(2 marks)**

Remember it!

- Variable costs change in line with the level of output.
- The more products that a business produces and sells, the higher the variable costs will be. If output doubles, then the variable costs will double.

Total costs `see pp. 71–72`

What you need to know

- Explain what is meant by total costs.
- Calculate total costs.

What are total costs?

Total costs are all the fixed costs and variable costs that a business incurs.

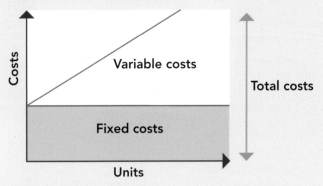

Calculating total costs per unit

Total costs per unit = total fixed costs per unit + total variable costs per unit

Example: During March a business has to pay £5000 fixed costs and £3500 variable costs. The business makes 50 units during the month.

Total costs per unit = total fixed costs per unit + total variable costs per unit

Total fixed costs per unit = £5000 ÷ 50
$\qquad\qquad\qquad\qquad$ = £100

Total variable costs per unit = £3500 ÷ 50
$\qquad\qquad\qquad\qquad\qquad$ = £70

Total costs per unit = £100 + £70 = £170

Calculating total costs for overall level of output

Total costs for a level of output
= total fixed costs + total variable costs

Example: Charlie makes 70 units in June. He pays £4500 fixed costs and £6800 variable costs.

The total costs for 70 units are: total fixed costs + total variable costs.

£4500 + £6800 = £11 300

Calculating total costs for a time period

- Total cost per month = total annual costs ÷ 12
- Total cost per year = total costs per month × 12

Examples: The total costs for Tia's business are £12 000 per year. Total costs per month = £12 000 ÷ 12 months = £1000

Total costs to operate RM Bikes are £5000 per month. Total cost per year = £5000 × 12 months = £60 000

Practise it!

The costs to run Ziggy's Barbers are as follows:

- fixed costs per year = £48 000
- variable costs per month = £3000

Calculate the total costs per month.   **(2 marks)**

Remember it!

- Total costs are all the costs to produce the product – they are the total of all the fixed and all the variable costs.
- Total costs can be expressed as a value for a level of output or per unit.

Revenue generated by sales see pp. 73–74

What you need to know

- Explain what is meant by revenue and how to calculate revenue.
- Rearrange the revenue formula to find a component and calculate revenue for different time periods.

Revenue is the amount of money that a business receives from selling its products.

Calculating total revenue

Total revenue = selling price per unit
× number sold

Example: A business sells stationery to schools. It starts by selling student planners for £4.99. In one year, the business sells 620 planners. Calculate the total revenue.

Selling price × number sold = total revenue

£4.99 × 620 = £3093.80

Using revenue to calculate selling price

Example: Stella sells 50 pens and makes £32.50 revenue. To find the selling price per pen:

Selling price per unit = total revenue
÷ number sold

Selling price per unit = £32.50 ÷ 50 = £0.65

Using revenue to calculate number of items sold

Example: Devon makes £50 revenue from selling doughnuts. He charges 50p per doughnut. To find the number of doughnuts sold:

Number sold = total revenue ÷ selling price

Number sold = £50 ÷ £0.50 = 100 doughnuts

Calculating revenue for different time periods

Example: Roy's business earns £600 revenue during an average month.

Revenue per year = £600 per month
× 12 months = £7200

Clara earns £12000 revenue per year from her business.

Revenue per month = £12000 ÷ 12 months
= £1000

Practise it!

1   Hannah sells cupcakes. She made £76.50 revenue at an event and charged 75p per cupcake. Calculate the number of cupcakes she sold. **(2 marks)**

2   Richie's car wash business washes 60 cars during an average week. He charges £6 per car. Calculate the total revenue generated by Richie's business each year. **(2 marks)**

Remember it!

- Revenue is the money a business receives from selling its products.
- The amount of revenue generated is affected by the number of products that the business sells and also the price charged for each product.

Profit and loss 1 see p. 75

What you need to know

- Explain what is meant by profit and loss.
- Rearrange the profit/loss formula to find a missing component.

What is profit?

Profit is the amount of money that a business/entrepreneur makes. It is calculated by subtracting the money spent (e.g. costs to produce a product and operate the business) from total revenue.

Why does a business need to make a profit?

- To survive.
- To reward the entrepreneur financially.
- To grow the business by reinvesting the profits.

How is profit for an overall level of output calculated?

Profit (or loss) = total revenue − total costs

Example: A business makes £600 revenue per month and has total costs (fixed costs + variable costs) of £300 per month.

Total revenue − total costs = profit (or loss)

£600 − £300 = £300

What is loss?

A **loss** is when a business's costs are greater than the revenue it generates from sales.

What could happen if a business makes a loss?

- The business cannot survive so it stops trading.
- The business cannot pay costs, e.g. wages.

It is possible for a business to make a loss occasionally, but it will not survive if it continues to make a loss over a long period of time.

Revise it!

Use index cards to write down various implications for a business if making a profit and a loss, e.g. the business can use the money to expand, or the business cannot pay costs such as wages. Write one implication on each card. Mix up the cards and then categorise them as to whether a business made a profit or a loss.

Remember it!

The formula to calculate the amount of profit or loss is the same. However, the answer will indicate if the business has generated a profit or loss. It will be positive if a profit has been made and negative if a loss.

Revision Guide

Profit and loss 2 see p. 75

- Explain what is meant by profit and loss.
- Rearrange the profit/loss formula to find a missing component.

How is profit per unit calculated?

Profit (or loss) per unit = revenue per unit − total costs per unit

Example: A business sells each item for £10 and the total costs per unit are £2.50.

Revenue per unit − total costs per unit = profit (or loss) per unit

£10 − £2.50 = £7.50

Rearranging the formula

It might be necessary to rearrange the formula to find out other figures, such as total costs.

Example: A business has total revenue of £1000 per month and a profit of £300 per month.

Total revenue − profit = total costs

£1000 − £300 = £700

Practise it!

1 Chuck generated £3689 revenue in May. His fixed costs were £1840 and variable costs were £1200. Calculate his profit in May. **(2 marks)**
2 Assuming May is an average month, calculate the profit/loss that Chuck makes each year. **(1 mark)**

Remember it!

Revenue and profit are *not* the same. Profit (or loss) is total revenue minus total costs. This is the amount of money the business makes (or loses).

Break-even see pp. 76–77

What you need to know

- Explain what is meant by and calculate break-even.
- Rearrange the break-even formula to find a missing component.

What is break-even?

Break-even point is the level of sales/output at which a business is making neither a profit nor a loss. The total costs are equal to the total revenue it is generating.

Break-even: total revenue = total costs

- **Break-even quantity**: the number of units that the business needs to sell in order to break even.
- **Break-even level of sales:** the level of sales at which the total costs are equal to the total revenue being generated.

Break-even calculations are normally carried out using forecasts or estimates about the future. The forecasted costs and revenue may be based on past figures and what the entrepreneur predicts they will be in the future.

Calculating break-even using a formula

$$\text{Break-even quantity (in units)} = \frac{\text{fixed costs}}{\text{selling price per unit} - \text{variable cost per unit}}$$

Example: A business sells coffee mugs. The price of each mug is £5. The business's fixed costs are £8000 per month. The variable costs to make a mug are £2.60.

Break-even quantity = £8000 ÷ (£5.00 − £2.60) = 3334 (answer rounded up to next whole number)

If the business sells 3330 mugs it will make a loss; however, if the business sells 3335 mugs it will make a profit.

Practise it!

1   Josh runs a greetings cards business. His fixed costs are £4000 per month. The average selling price per card is £2.50. The variable cost per card is 90p. If he sells 2850 cards in June, will he make a profit or a loss? **(3 marks)**

2   How much profit/loss will Josh make in June? **(1 mark)**

Remember it!

- Break-even point is the level of sales/output at which a business is neither making a profit nor a loss.
- The figures used to calculate the break-even point are normally forecasts or estimates, so they may not be accurate.

Interpreting a break-even graph see p. 78

- Identify figures and lines in a break-even graph.

A break-even graph is a visual way of showing the break-even quantity.

What does a break-even graph show?

- There are three lines on a break-even graph:
  - fixed costs
  - total costs.
  - total revenue
- Axes:
  - x axis (horizontal) = number of units
  - y axis (vertical) = costs/revenue.
- Break-even is the point where the total revenue line and total cost line cross.
- The blue shaded area (to the left of the break-even point) shows where the business will make a loss.
- The pink shaded area (to the right of the break-even point) shows where the business will make a profit.

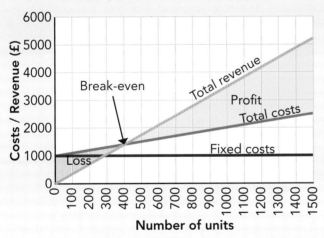

The break-even graph shows that the business needs to sell 400 units to break even.

Interpreting a break-even graph

When interpreting a break-even graph, remember that the:

- **fixed costs** line is a straight horizontal line
- **total costs** line starts at the same point as the fixed cost line because even at a level of zero output, fixed costs are incurred
- **total revenue** line starts at zero and goes up diagonally as the number of units increases
- **break-even point** is the point where the total cost and total revenue lines cross.

Using break-even information

An entrepreneur may use the information to:

- make decisions on how many units they need to sell to make a profit
- support an application for a bank loan or to get investment
- identify any costs that the business needs to reduce
- decide what price to charge for a product.

The break-even graph can be changed to show the impact of reducing costs and changing the price.

---

1 State the names of the *three* lines on a break-even graph. **(3 marks)**
2 Identify *two* decisions that break-even can help an entrepreneur make. **(2 marks)**

- A break-even graph is a visual way of showing the break-even quantity.
- Break-even is the point where the total revenue line and total cost line cross on the graph.
- Three lines are plotted on a break-even graph.

The importance of cash see p. 79

What you need to know

- Explain what is meant by cash and the difference between cash and profit.
- Explain why a business needs cash and what might happen if it does not have enough.

What is cash?

Cash is the physical money (notes and coins) that a business holds in a till or its bank account that is readily available to pay any debts or expenses.

Cash flowing into the business   **Cash flowing out of the business**

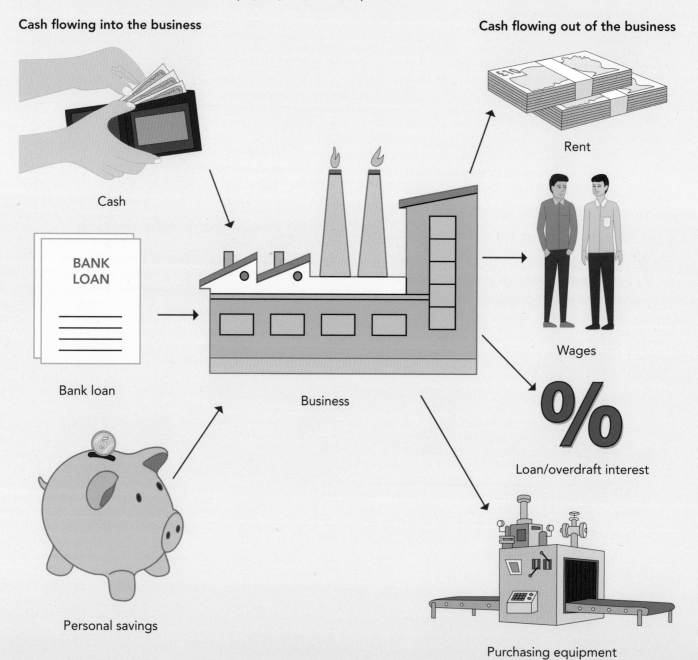

Cash

Bank loan

Personal savings

Business

Rent

Wages

Loan/overdraft interest

Purchasing equipment

The business must always have enough cash, i.e. the amount of money coming into a business must be greater than the amount of money going out of the business. Businesses must take care with their cash flow as it changes constantly.

Why do businesses need cash?

Without sufficient cash, a business is unable to:

- pay its bills (e.g. utilities) and employees' wages/salaries
- repay debts and loans
- buy materials to make products.

If a business is unable to pay its bills it will not survive for very long.

Other businesses and people that it owes money to might take legal action to force the business to pay the outstanding bills. This could result in the business being forced to close.

Cash versus profit

Cash is **not** profit.

> **Profit = total revenue − total costs**

A profitable business may not have enough cash to pay its bills because some customers might not pay for products or services immediately. They might delay paying for as long as possible.

Practise it!

1   Which of the following best describes cash? Tick (✓) the correct answer. **(1 mark)**

   a   Money in the business's bank account/till ☐

   b   Total revenue ☐

   c   All of the business's costs ☐

   d   Total revenue minus total costs ☐

2   Explain *one* reason why a business needs to have cash. **(2 marks)**

3   Explain *one* consequence of not having enough cash. **(2 marks)**

Remember it!

- Cash is the physical money that a business has in the bank or in the till. A business needs cash in order to operate.

- A business that does not have enough cash will be unable to pay its bills and may have to stop trading.

The marketing mix see p. 80

What you need to know

- Outline the four elements of the marketing mix: price, product, place and promotion.
- Explain how these elements work together.

The **marketing mix** is made up of four elements – the 4Ps – that are needed to successfully sell a product and meet customers' needs. The right product must be sold at the right price and in the right place. Successful promotion supports this.

1 Product

The product must meet the needs of the customers.

Who is the product targeted at?

What features do customers want?

How does it stand out from other similar products? Does it have a clear USP?

2 Price

The price must reflect what customers are willing and able to pay.

It must also cover the costs of production so that the business makes a profit.

3 Place

Where the product is sold.

Businesses need to consider the best place to sell the product, e.g. in:

- a physical shop or online
- a way to suit the rest of the marketing mix, e.g. a luxury product in an exclusive store with fewer outlets.

4 Promotion

Communicating the product's features and benefits to the customer.

Making customers aware of products, e.g. by advertising and sales promotions.

Using the right promotional method is important, e.g. giving out leaflets might be more suitable for a local business.

How the marketing mix works together

All of the 4Ps must work together. They must also be aimed at the same target market. For example, selling a basic product at a high price and advertising it in a high-end magazine will not be effective because customers will not pay a high price for a basic product, and readers of high-end magazines are unlikely to buy a basic product.

Practise it!

1 Identify the *four* elements of the marketing mix. **(4 marks)**

2 Explain why a high price may not be suitable for an economy can of baked beans sold by a discount retailer. **(2 marks)**

Remember it!

- The marketing mix consists of the 4Ps – price, product, place and promotion.
- All elements must work together as they affect one another – e.g. you cannot charge a high price for a product and sell it in a store that sells economy products.

Non-digital advertising mediums 1 see pp. 81–82

What you need to know

- Identify and explain non-digital advertising methods that businesses use.
- Analyse the advantages and disadvantages of each non-digital medium.

Non-digital advertising mediums are more 'traditional' methods that do not rely on technology.

Leaflets

- Printed pieces of paper to advertise and offer key information about a product.
- Often used by local businesses to target local areas.
- Handed out in the street, displayed on a stand or posted through letter boxes.

Advantages	Disadvantages
• Easy to read • Give the customer a physical advert to keep • Relatively cheap to produce. Images and colour can increase or decrease costs • Effective for targeting a local area	• Many people do not read them, seeing them as 'junk mail' • Can be time-consuming to distribute • Environmental cost of printing leaflets (use of paper) • Leaflets often only have a short-term impact

Newspapers

- Local newspapers cover local areas; national newspapers cover the whole country.
- The cost of advertising depends on the type of newspaper; readership; size and colour of the advert; and location of the advert – some pages are more expensive to advertise.

Advantages	Disadvantages
• Can target a specific market segment based on its readership • Readers can keep a physical copy of the advert for future reference • Can use colour, headings, photos and graphics to increase the impact • The cost of advertising in local and free newspapers may be relatively low	• Are more likely to be read by an older audience, making it a less effective method of reaching younger target customers • Can be expensive (e.g. if large and in colour) • Content does not move and is not interactive • Adverts may not be seen if there are lots of them on one page, or people may not read them

Magazines

- Magazine advertising can be used to target a specific market segment.

Revise it!

Flash cards: Create a flash card for each of the six non-digital advertising mediums. Describe the medium on the front of the card. On the reverse, add the advantages and disadvantages. Revisit these regularly to test your knowledge.

Remember it!

- Cost is an important factor when assessing the advantages and disadvantages of different mediums.
- The cost of leaflets and newspaper and magazine adverts can depend on size, number of images, and whether they are colour or black and white.

Non-digital advertising mediums 2 see pp. 83–84

What you need to know

- Identify and explain non-digital advertising methods that businesses use to inform customers about products.
- Analyse the advantages and disadvantages of each non-digital medium.

- Many magazines are targeted at specific groups, e.g. by gender, by interest, by age and by occupation.

Advantages	Disadvantages
• Can target specific market segments by advertising in magazines related to the readers' interests, gender, etc. • If magazines are published monthly the advert will have a longer impact than in some other mediums • Can use colour, headings, photos etc. to increase impact • Are widely shared (e.g. in doctors' waiting rooms, hairdressers, between friends and family) which increases the number of people who see the advert	• Readers may skip adverts and focus on the articles • Mostly target a national audience so are not suitable for local products/services • Adverts are often expensive • May not be seen if there are lots of adverts on one page

Radio

- There are a number of local and national commercial radio stations.
- Between programmes they have commercial breaks that contain adverts. Adverts are sold in 30-second slots.
- Adverts include jingles, speech and music.

Advantages	Disadvantages
• Local adverts target customers in a specific geographical area • The time and station on which the advert is broadcast can be chosen to target specific listeners • Catchy jingles/phrases can grab listeners' attention and become well known and associated with the brand	• Listeners may not take in all of the key information • The advert may be less than a minute long, limiting the amount of detailed information that can be included • Many listeners are 'passive' listeners and either change stations during the adverts or have the radio on in the background, e.g. in the car • Production costs may be high • Adverts at peak listening times are more expensive

Practise it!

1 Explain *one* advantage of advertising in a magazine. **(2 marks)**
2 Explain *one* disadvantage of radio advertising. (2 marks) **(2 marks)**

Remember it!

- Non-digital advertising mediums can be an effective way to reach a range of target customers.

Non-digital advertising mediums 3 see pp. 81–84

What you need to know

- Identify and explain non-digital advertising methods that businesses use to inform customers about products.
- Analyse the advantages and disadvantages of each non-digital medium.

Posters/billboards

- Poster and billboards are a visual way of advertising.
- Billboards are enlarged versions of posters and can be either static or digital.
- Digital billboards have moving images and often have multiple adverts on them.

Advantages	Disadvantages
• Posters are relatively cheap to produce and can be very eye catching • Posters can be effective if they are placed in a location that is accessed by the target customer	• Customers may miss key information if they are passing the poster or billboard quickly, e.g. in a car • Prime locations are expensive • Billboards often cost more than posters because they have to be professionally designed and put up

Cinema

- Cinema screens are large screens with maximum input in terms of sound and visuals.
- Adverts are normally shown for 20–30 minutes before the film begins.

Advantages	Disadvantages
• Businesses can target customers by advertising when the target audience for the film matches the target audience for the product • Cinema adverts cost less than TV adverts, but they have moving images and audio on a large screen for impact	• They are expensive to produce and are likely to be too expensive for smaller businesses • Many cinema goers arrive after the adverts or talk during them, so they miss them

Practise it!

1 Explain *one* disadvantage of advertising a new soft drink in the cinema. **(2 marks)**

2 Explain *one* advantage of a fast food restaurant advertising a new vegan burger on a billboard. **(2 marks)**

Remember it!

- Posters/billboards and cinema advertising can have real audio-visual impact.
- However, people may not engage with the advert if they are doing something else, so they may not remember it.

Digital advertising mediums 1 see pp. 81–82

What you need to know

- Identify and explain digital advertising methods that businesses use to attract and retain customers as well as inform customers about products.
- Analyse the advantages and disadvantages of each digital medium.

Digital advertising mediums use digital technology and the internet to target customers of all ages – not just younger ones.

Social media

- Adverts use social media platforms, such as Facebook and Instagram.
- Many businesses set up business accounts on the different social media platforms and post updates regularly (e.g. photos, videos, product information, reviews, offers).
- A business must choose appropriate platforms based on the target customer.

Advantages	Disadvantages
• Customers who follow the business are likely to be interested in the advert/product • These adverts are cheaper than more traditional methods of advertising • The business can interact with customers around the world through comments and sharing	• Customers can leave negative and inappropriate comments which can damage the business's reputation • Customers expect regular posts and prompt responses. This can be time-consuming for a small business

SMS texts

- Adverts that are sent in bulk by text message to customers who have given their mobile phone number to the business.

Advantages	Disadvantages
• Customers have already provided their details and they have an interest in the business • This is a low-cost way of advertising • Businesses can track people who take up the offer, purchase or visit the website by clicking the link in the message	• Messages can only be short and have a limited number of words • Some customers get annoyed by the texts and ignore them, and they may opt out of receiving future texts • Customer contact details might change without the business knowing

Revise it!

Create a mind map of the digital advertising methods here and on Digital advertising mediums 2 and 3. Add all of the advantages of the methods in one colour and all of the disadvantages in another colour.

Over time, recreate the mind map but reduce the number of words to make it easier to remember.

Remember it!

- Digital advertising is important as entrepreneurs can reach lots of people of all ages around the world.
- However, a business cannot assume that all of its target market has access to the internet or is confident using it (e.g. non-technically minded people).

Revision Guide

Digital advertising mediums 2 see pp. 83–84

What you need to know

- Identify and explain digital advertising methods that businesses use to attract and retain customers as well as inform customers about products.
- Analyse the advantages and disadvantages of each digital medium.

Websites

- A website provides pictures and information about a business's products and services.
- Most businesses need to have an online presence through:
  - their own website
  - selling/advertising on a third-party website such as eBay or Etsy.
- Websites are linked to search engines so that they appear when a customer does a search.

Advantages	Disadvantages
• Customers can access a website from anywhere in the world at any time of the day • Websites are relatively economical to build and they are easy to update with new products, price changes, etc. • Businesses can sell products via their own website or through a third-party website	• Some people do not have access to the internet, or technical issues can prevent access • A business may need specialist help to build the website and attract visitors, which can be costly • A website needs to be maintained so that it is up to date, which can be time-consuming

Banners and pop-ups

- Banners appear on websites belonging to someone else and stay visible while a user is on that page.
- Pop-ups appear temporarily on top of another web page before disappearing or being removed by the user.

Advantages	Disadvantages
• These can be static or moving images. Some also contain music to catch users' attention • Businesses can target customers effectively by placing banners/pop-ups on websites that are relevant to the target customer • They are relatively low cost	• People get irritated by pop-ups and do not read them before closing them • They can only contain a small amount of information

Revise it!

Flash cards: Create a flash card for each of the six digital advertising mediums. Describe the medium on the front of the card. On the reverse, draw small pictures to represent the advantages and disadvantages. Revisit these regularly to test your knowledge.

Remember it!

- Most businesses have a website to promote their products and/or sell products.
- The content within a digital advert is often easier to change, which means that the information is more up to date.

Digital advertising mediums 3 see pp. 81–84

What you need to know

- Identify and explain digital advertising methods that businesses use to attract and retain customers as well as inform customers about products.
- Analyse the advantages and disadvantages of each digital medium.

Podcasts

- Pre-recorded audio and video on the internet that discusses a specific topic. The **podcast** can be:
  - a one-off, to promote a product, or
  - part of another podcast (e.g. by an influencer) discussing a new product or an existing product.

Advantages	Disadvantages
• Podcasts can be created easily and cheaply using a smartphone or a computer • They can link with other forms of advertising, such as promoting the podcast on a website or through social media or including the radio advert jingle in the podcast • They can be linked to an 'influencer' to increase popularity	• Podcasts are more effective when they are part of a series of podcasts, which takes more time and effort to create • Customers may be too busy to listen to podcasts

Vlogs/blogs

- Blogs are written forms of advertising that discuss a product.
- **Vlogs** are video blogs often distributed through platforms like YouTube.
- Both are published regularly to build a following.

Advantages	Disadvantages
• Vlogs and blogs can be used to discuss products or aspects of a business to help build relationships with customers • They can provide detailed information about products and give the customer an opportunity to interact through comments • Specific people can be targeted via an influencer's blog/vlog	• It can be too time-consuming for a small business to create vlogs or blogs as well as other advertising • Some customers may not have time to engage with longer vlogs/blogs • A professional vlog can be expensive to produce

Practise it!

1. State *one* disadvantage of a vlog. **(1 mark)**
2. Analyse *two* benefits of advertising through digital mediums. **(6 marks)**

Remember it!

Digital advertising is less expensive than other traditional non-digital methods. However, it is not free and it is not accessible to everyone. It can also be time-consuming to create.

Sales promotion techniques 1 see p. 85

- Identify examples of sales promotion techniques.
- Understand the appropriateness of a specific sales promotion technique.
- Analyse the benefits and limitations of specific sales promotion techniques.

Sales promotion techniques help to attract and retain customers.

Discounts

A discount is when a business reduces the price of the product, such as 50 percent off or 50p off the price. Discounts are used for a short period of time only.

Advantages	Disadvantages
• Customers see the product as a bargain and are tempted to try it • Sales may increase for the period of the promotion and create brand loyalty	• There is no guarantee of brand loyalty • Customers may only purchase the product while the discount is offered • The amount of revenue generated reduces • The product might be seen as low quality

Competitions

The customer interacts with the business with the aim of winning a prize.

Advantages	Disadvantages
• This guarantees engagement between the customer and the business • High-value prizes tempt customers to purchase • Competitions can generate publicity and product awareness	• Prizes have to be something the customer wants • They can be costly to the business, e.g. the cost of running the competition and providing the prize • The competition must be promoted so that customers are aware of it

Buy one, get one free (BOGOF)

Customers purchase one product and get another identical product for free.

Advantages	Disadvantages
• Customers see the product as a bargain and will try it • Customers have twice as much of the product to try. This can lead to brand loyalty	• It is costly to give away products for free and can reduce the business's profit margin • BOGOF can encourage wastage as customers may not need a second product

Revise it!

Create some small cards. On one side of the card write a benefit/limitation of one of the sales promotion techniques, and then write the name of the sales promotion technique on the other side. Select a card at random and read the benefit/limitation; then name the sales promotion technique. Turn over the card to see the answer.

Remember it!

- Discounts and BOGOFs encourage customers to try a product, but they can be seen as 'cheapening' the product/brand and some customers may only purchase while the offer runs.
- Competitions help the business/brand to engage with customers, but prizes can be costly.

Sales promotion techniques 2 see p. 85

What you need to know

- Identify examples of sales promotion techniques.
- Understand the appropriateness of a specific sales promotion technique.
- Analyse the benefits and limitations of specific sales promotion techniques.

Point-of-sale advertising

Banners, posters and displays at the till (the point of sale) can encourage customers to make an impulse purchase, e.g.:

- a display of chocolate
- a poster (printed or on a digital screen by the till) that advertises products
- a pop-up stating: 'Other people who purchased these products also bought...'

Advantages	Disadvantages
• It encourages customers to buy additional low-cost items • It is simple and cheap to organise/ prepare a display	• It is not suitable for high-cost items as people do not impulse buy high-cost goods • As point-of-sale items are low cost, this generates low revenue • Most retailers have limited space for point-of-sale advertising, so only a small range of products can benefit

Loyalty schemes

Customers collect points or stamps on a card each time they shop. Points can be exchanged for a reward (e.g. a free gift or money off).

The schemes allow larger businesses to collect useful customer data, e.g. customers' buying habits and patterns.

Advantages	Disadvantages
• Data collected from the loyalty scheme helps the business predict and track consumer habits and make marketing decisions • Customers remain loyal and keep returning to collect their rewards • They allow the business to target customers with special offers	• Many businesses, big and small, offer loyalty schemes so it is difficult to make a scheme stand out • Customers will only engage and remain loyal if the reward is worthwhile • They can be costly to operate as the business may need to purchase or upgrade IT systems

Revise it!

Add one fact about sales promotion techniques to a sticky note. Keep writing points on sticky notes until you have covered all of the key facts. Stick the notes in prominent places and read them regularly. You will take in the information without realising.

Remember it!

- Point-of-sale advertising is commonly used to encourage customers to make low-cost impulse purchases.
- Loyalty cards are a way of encouraging repeat custom so that customers can accumulate more rewards, and they allow businesses to collect data about customers to help plan future marketing.

Sales promotion techniques 3 see p. 85

- Identify examples of sales promotion techniques.
- Understand the appropriateness of a specific sales promotion technique.
- Analyse the benefits and limitations of specific sales promotion techniques.

Sponsorship

Sponsorship is when a business supports an event, a team or a TV show financially in return for advertising. For example, Coca-Cola sponsors McLaren in Formula 1.

Advantages	Disadvantages
• Businesses benefit from a raised public profile and brand awareness • The business can be seen as 'kind' or 'generous' by the general public • The business may be associated with positive aspects of the event/activity it sponsors, e.g. a health drink or low-fat spread sponsoring a sporting event	• There is no guarantee that sponsorship will lead to increased sales • If the team or individual that is sponsored receives bad publicity it can affect the brand

Free gifts and product trials

The customer receives a free gift when they buy a product, e.g. a shower gel for free when buying a perfume, or a free toy with a fast-food meal. With a product trial, a small sample of a product is handed out for customers to try, e.g. food and drink in a supermarket.

Advantages	Disadvantages
• Free gifts can persuade a customer to purchase from one company rather than another • Customers try an additional product that they may buy in future • Product trials allow customers to try the product. If they like it, they are more likely to buy it in future • Businesses can gather customer feedback with product trials	• Customers must value the free gift otherwise there will not be an incentive to buy • The cost of offering a free gift can be high • There is no guarantee that people will purchase following the product trial • It can be expensive to give away free products in a trial • Competitors can see the product in the trial before it is launched

Practise it!

1 Explain *one* reason why an organisation may use a sales promotion technique. **(2 marks)**

2 Explain *two* limitations of using point-of-sale (POS) techniques. **(4 marks)**

Remember it!

The goal of all sales promotion techniques is to increase revenue for the business. However, they can be costly for a business, so they are only used in the short term.

Public relations (PR) see p. 85

What you need to know

- Explain what PR is and how it can be used to benefit a business.
- Analyse the relative benefits and limitations of specific PR methods.

Public relations (PR) is about promoting the company's reputation and building a positive relationship with the customer without directly advertising the brand. See PR methods below:

1 Product Placement
Branded products are placed in well-known TV shows and films (e.g. Etch-A-Sketch in *Toy Story*)

Advantages
- People see the product as part of the film/TV show and don't realise it is being advertised.
- People link positive feelings about a brand with the TV show/film.

Disadvantages
- Expensive, so unaffordable for small businesses.
- Product might not be remembered if other brands appear in the same film/TV show.

2 Celebrity endorsement
Uses a celebrity's fame to promote a product or brand (e.g. Gary Lineker and Walkers crisps)

Advantages
- A celebrity provides customers with a recognisable face and builds trust.
- A product/brand linked to a celebrity is more likely to be recognised.

Disadvantages
- Very expensive to get a celebrity to endorse a product.
- If the celebrity misbehaves, it can impact on the brand's reputation.

3 Press/media release
An important news story about the company/its products that is sent to the local media (e.g. local newspaper or radio station)

Advantages
- Free publicity.
- Can target specific customers by targeting a particular newspaper/radio station.

Disadvantages
- Story won't be featured if it is not engaging/of interest to the readers/listeners.
- Story may be misinterpreted by journalists, which could change the emphasis/facts.

Practise it!

1. Identify *two* public relations methods that a business may use. **(2 marks)**
2. Analyse *two* benefits to your school of sending a press release to the local newspaper to promote the opening of a new science block. **(6 marks)**

Remember it!

- There are three methods of public relations – product placement, **celebrity endorsement** and **press/media releases**.
- Public relations aims to create a **positive** image of the brand and get customers' attention without openly advertising the brand.

How to sell goods and services see pp. 86–87

What you need to know

- Explain how businesses can sell products to their customers.
- Analyse the advantages and disadvantages of physical and digital channels.

Making products available to customers in the right place and at the right time is an important part of the marketing mix. Entrepreneurs must decide whether to sell their goods or services through physical or digital locations or a mix of both.

Physical

- **Shops** – the product is sold in a physical shop (e.g. an independent shop, a salon or a series of bigger stores across a region/country).
- **Face to face** – the owner or employees interact directly with the customers (e.g. in a shop or at a product demonstration).

Advantages	Disadvantages
• Develops relationships between the customer and the business • Customers can physically see and touch a product • Staff are able to explain products to customers	• The costs of a physical store can be very expensive (e.g. rent, wages, etc.) • Most shops are not open 24 hours a day, which is less convenient for customers

Digital

- **E-commerce/websites** – the product is sold via the business's or a third-party website.
- **Social media** – sharing news and promotions about a product which link to the business's website.
- **Marketplace sites** – websites which offer products from different sellers, e.g. Facebook.
- **Online auction sites** – websites where customers bid on products, e.g. eBay.
- **Downloads** – digital products or files can be purchased or downloaded immediately through a download store (e.g. the Google Play Store).

Advantages	Disadvantages
• Fewer costs than physical stores • Lower costs can mean a lower product price or increased profit margin • Flexibility for the customer as they can buy 24 hours a day • Can serve customers over a wider geographic area	• Customers must wait to receive their goods • Customers cannot always get an immediate response from the business if they have queries • Customers cannot interact with the product and ask questions

Practise it!

1 Explain *one* reason why more businesses are switching to digital channels. **(2 marks)**

2 Analyse *one* advantage to a high street bank of continuing to serve customers face to face in a branch. **(3 marks)**

Remember it!

- Businesses may have a physical location or an online presence.
- Businesses often have a mixture of both to ensure that they meet the needs of all customers.

The product lifecycle 1 see pp. 88–89

- Identify the five stages of the product life cycle and explain the features of each stage.
- Explain how the marketing mix may be adapted for each stage of the product lifecycle.

The **product lifecycle** shows the different stages that a product goes through from development to withdrawal from the market. It helps businesses to make appropriate marketing mix decisions.

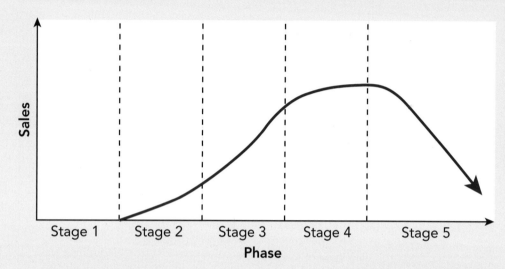

Stages

1 Development
2 Introduction
3 Growth
4 Maturity
5 Decline

1. Development

- Market research is carried out.
- The product is developed and tested.

Promotion: None – as there is no product to promote.

Sales and profit: No sales/profit. Can start a pre-order system to generate some income.

2. Introduction

- The product is launched onto the market.
- Different price strategies are used to attract customers.

Promotion: High levels of promotion to make customers aware of the new product.

Price: The product may be launched with a high or low price depending on the type of product and pricing strategy used.

Sales and profit: Sales increase slowly for most products. The business is likely to make a loss due to the development costs of creating the product.

Revise it!

Create some revision cards. On half of the cards, write the stages of the product lifecycle. On the rest of the cards write a description of the key features of each stage of the product lifecycle, e.g. sales, profits, promotion and price.

Mix up the description cards and then match them to the product lifecycle stage card that they relate to.

Remember it!

The entrepreneur is unlikely to generate high profits during the first two stages of the product lifecycle due to:

- the costs of developing the product
- relatively low sales as customers are yet to become aware of the product.

The product lifecycle 2 see pp. 88–89

- Identify the five stages of the product life cycle and explain the features of each stage.
- Explain how the marketing mix may be adapted for each stage of the product lifecycle.

3. Growth

- Customers are more aware of the product.
- It is sold in more locations.
- Competitors start to make similar products.

Promotion: Promotion costs are high. High levels of promotion strengthen brand image and increase market share.

Price: The price may increase/decrease gradually as customers adopt the product more widely.

Sales and profit: A rapid increase in sales leading to improved profitability.

4. Maturity

- Most people have already bought the product.
- Repeat customers continue to buy the product.
- Strong competition from other products.

Promotion: Sales promotions are used to retain customers, attract customers from competitors and remain competitive.

Price: The price is likely to be in line with that of competitors.

Sales and profit: Sales peak and level off as most people already have the product. Profits stabilise.

5. Decline

- Product is outdated.
- Reduced customer demand.
- Some competitors leave the market.

Promotion: Little money is spent on promotion.

Price: The price may be reduced to maintain customer demand. It may increase if other competitors have left the market and it is the only product remaining on the market.

Sales and profit: Sales fall. The product may continue to be sold to loyal customers at a loss. Or, if it is the only product left on the market after competitors have left, it may be sold at a higher price thereby making a profit.

Practise it!

1 The table shows the sales of four products. Identify which stage of the product lifecycle each product is in. **(4 marks)**

Product	Number of products sold			
	Year 1	Year 2	Year 3	Year 4
A	0	0	0	12
B	450	420	350	250
C	0	15	90	150
D	650	670	675	675

2 Analyse why the profit generated by Product A may be very low. **(3 marks)**

Remember it!

- The product lifecycle has **five** stages: development, introduction, growth, maturity and decline.
- While all products will go through this lifecycle, the amount of time spent in each stage will vary from product to product. The lifecycle for some products will be weeks whereas other products remain popular for decades.

Extension strategies 1 see pp. 88–89

- Identify extension strategies for products with reference to the product lifecycle.
- Explain extension strategies that a business can use to lengthen a product's life.

Price changes

Advantages	Disadvantages
Reducing the price: • new customers may try the product as it is more affordable • existing customers are more likely to buy again • customers may switch from competitor products if the price is lower Increasing the price: • generates more revenue and profit • may help the product to appear more luxurious	Reducing the price: • could harm the product's reputation as it could be seen as being lower quality • may not be enough to encourage customers to buy, so it may not generate extra sales • reduces revenue Increasing the price: • customers expect a higher-quality product • customers might not be willing or able to pay more

Advertising

Advantages	Disadvantages
• Reminds existing customers of the product's features and benefits • May attract new customers • Can help to build brand loyalty	• Advertising campaigns can be expensive • No guarantee that it will lead to more sales • May only lead to a short-term increase in sales while the campaign is running

Adding value

This involves changing a product to include a new feature or a function.

Advantages	Disadvantages
• The business can charge a higher price for the improved product and increase revenue • The product might be more desirable to customers, resulting in increased sales • Can make the product stand out from the competition	• Customers might not be interested in the new features or won't pay the increased price • Expensive to research, develop and advertise the new features

Revise it!

Record it! Read out loud the pages about product lifecycle extension strategies. You could record them using the voice recorder on your phone. Play the recordings to yourself regularly.

Remember it!

- **Extension strategies** are used to prevent the product from going into the decline stage.
- They aim to generate more sales, which will increase revenue and profits by renewing interest amongst the target market or attracting a new target market.

Extension strategies 2 see pp. 88–89

- Identify extension strategies for products with reference to the product lifecycle.
- Explain extension strategies that a business can use to lengthen a product's life.

Exploring new markets

A business may decide to sell its existing product into a different market, such as:

- in a new location/region/country (e.g. a business selling in the north-east of England might decide to sell its product across the whole of the UK)
- to a different market segment (e.g. a ladies' clothing retailer may introduce a children's range).

Advantages	Disadvantages
<ul><li>Can target different markets, which can increase market share</li><li>Being in several markets can spread risk, e.g. if one market declines the business can still benefit from another</li><li>Sales and profits may increase</li></ul>	<ul><li>Some products are not successful in other markets (e.g. they do not fit with the culture or beliefs)</li><li>Can be costly to set up in a new market because:<ul><li>new advertising is needed</li><li>changes to the product are required</li><li>market research can be expensive</li></ul></li></ul>

New packaging

Packaging for the product is changed by:

- refreshing it with a new design (e.g. new colours, logos, etc.)
- going back to an older, more traditional design of packaging to attract previous customers who remember the original packaging.

Advantages	Disadvantages
<ul><li>Makes customers think that the product has been updated/improved</li><li>Updated packaging might make the product stand out more from competing products</li><li>May help the product to appeal to a new market</li></ul>	<ul><li>May be expensive to design and produce packaging</li><li>Stock in older packaging might have to be withdrawn or sold at a discount</li><li>Customers may not recognise the new packaging</li><li>Customers may be disappointed if the product has not changed</li></ul>

Practise it!

1 Explain two extension strategies that you think a soft-drinks business could consider to stop the decline of a previously best-selling drink and increase sales. **(4 marks)**

2 Analyse the advantages and disadvantages of each of the two extension strategies you selected in Question 1. **(6 marks)**

3 Recommend which of the two extension strategies will be most appropriate for the drink. Justify your answer. **(8 marks)**

Remember it!

- Each extension strategy is not used on its own.
- A business will often use a number of them at the same time to successfully extend the life of a product (e.g. new packaging and a new advertising campaign will help customers recognise the updated product).

Factors to consider when pricing a product see pp. 90–92

What you need to know

- Explain the factors to consider when pricing a product.

1. Income levels of target customers

- People will only be able to pay what they can afford, e.g. someone on a low income may only be able to afford a small second-hand car rather than a brand-new car.
- Customers must also value the product.

2. Price of competitor products

- Customers will not pay a high price if they are able to buy the same or a similar product from a competitor for less.
- If the product is better quality than the competitors' products, customers may be prepared to pay more for it.

3. Cost of production

- The selling price needs to cover the costs of making the product (fixed and variable costs) in order to make a profit rather than a loss.
- Selling price = production costs + profit. For example, if a product costs £5 to produce and the entrepreneur wants to make a £4 profit on each product, the selling price must be £9.

4. Stages of the product lifecycle

The stage of the product lifecycle will determine the price the business can charge.

Introduction	Growth	Maturity	Decline
A low price may attract buyers to purchase a new product and try it. Premium products (e.g. phones, TVs, etc.) might start with a high selling price as they are seen as desirable/luxurious.	The price may increase if the product had a low introductory price. If the introductory price was high, the price might be reduced to increase interest.	As sales level off, the price is brought in line with competitors' prices (as long as the product can still make a profit). This prevents the competitors from taking market share.	Sales are falling so the price is reduced to stimulate demand.

Practise it!

Explain why a business needs to consider the income of its target audience when setting a price for a product. **(2 marks)**

Remember it!

- The price of a product is affected by four factors: the stage of the product lifecycle, the income of target customers, the price of competitors' products and the cost of production.
- All four factors must be considered equally.

Pricing strategies see pp. 90–92

What you need to know

- Identify the four pricing strategies that businesses use.
- Recommend a pricing strategy for a specific start-up situation.

A **pricing strategy** is the method that businesses use to set a selling price for a product or service.

Competitive pricing

A business sets a price in line with that of its competitors.

Advantages	Disadvantages
• Competitors are not able to use price as a way of making their product stand out • The business knows that the customers are willing to pay this price	• Limits the amount of profit and may not cover the cost of production • Difficult to keep up with competitors' prices, especially on a global scale

Psychological pricing

A business sets a price which makes the customer think the item is cheaper.

Advantages	Disadvantages
• Limited impact on revenue as the difference is minimal (e.g. 1p per product) • Customers think the product is cheaper so they are more likely to buy	• Customers are aware of the strategy • Does not guarantee increased sales if customers do not consider the price difference to be enough

Price skimming

Selling a product at a high price to create interest when it is first introduced. The price is then reduced over time as new products are launched or competitors enter the market.

Advantages	Disadvantages
• Break-even point is lowered because fewer products need to be sold at a higher price to break even • Creates the impression that the product is better quality	• Some customers cannot afford to pay the higher price or may not be willing to pay it • Revenue is reduced if customers are not willing to pay a higher price

Price penetration

A low introductory price encourages customers to take a risk and try the new product. The price increases over time as the number of customers and market share grow.

Advantages	Disadvantages
• A low price encourages customers to try the product • A low price can create loyal customers who are willing to pay the higher price when it increases	• The business might make a loss or a low profit initially • There is no guarantee that customers will continue to purchase when the price rises

Practise it!

1 Explain *one* advantage of a price penetration strategy for a company which is launching a new product range in a new market. **(2 marks)**
2 Identify *three* disadvantages of a price penetration strategy. **(3 marks)**

Remember it!

There are four pricing strategies:

- **competitive pricing**
- **psychological pricing**
- **price skimming**
- **price penetration**.

Forms of business ownership 1 see pp. 93–94

What you need to know

- Identify appropriate forms of ownership for start-up businesses.
- Analyse the relative advantages and disadvantages of each form of ownership.

When starting up a business, an entrepreneur needs to decide on a form of ownership. This will influence decision making, how profits are shared and responsibility for debts.

Sole trader

- Owned and operated by *one* person.
- They make all of the key decisions and are responsible for the day-to-day running of the business.
- The most common form of business ownership in the UK.

Examples: plumber, gardener, hairdresser

Ownership: one owner – but can employ others

Liability: unlimited

Decision making: sole trader has 100 percent responsibility

Profits: sole trader keeps **all** profits

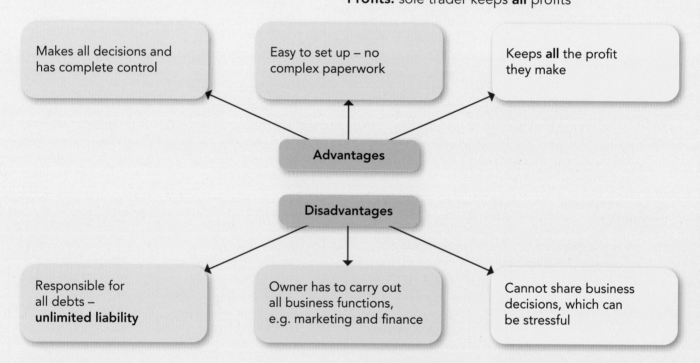

Makes all decisions and has complete control

Easy to set up – no complex paperwork

Keeps **all** the profit they make

Advantages

Disadvantages

Responsible for all debts – **unlimited liability**

Owner has to carry out all business functions, e.g. marketing and finance

Cannot share business decisions, which can be stressful

Revise it!

Create a mind map of key facts about each method of ownership (e.g. ownership, examples, liability, decision making and profit sharing). Add to it for each of the forms of ownership here and on Forms of business ownership 2, 3 and 4. Revisit this mind map regularly and recreate it, narrowing down the information so it shows just key points.

Remember it!

Sole traders have unlimited liability. This means that if they fail, the owner(s) must pay back the debts using their own personal money.

Forms of business ownership 2 see p. 95

What you need to know

- Identify appropriate forms of ownership for start-up businesses.
- Analyse the relative advantages and disadvantages of each form of ownership.

Partnership

- Owned and operated by *two or more people*.
- Decision making and profits are shared based on the terms in the **partnership agreement**.
- Each partner brings their own expertise.
- **Examples:** electrician, small grocery shop

- **Ownership:** *two* or more owners
- **Liability:** unlimited
- **Decision making:** split equally between the partners
- **Profits:** split equally between the partners

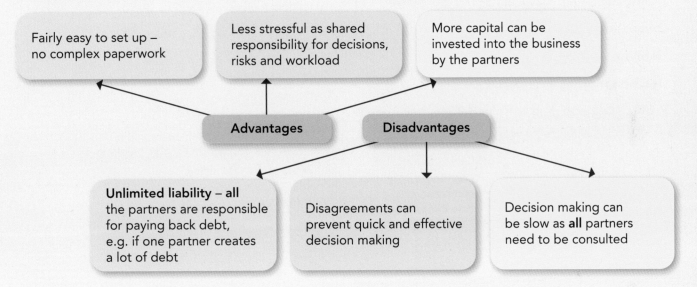

Fairly easy to set up – no complex paperwork

Less stressful as shared responsibility for decisions, risks and workload

More capital can be invested into the business by the partners

Advantages

Disadvantages

Unlimited liability – all the partners are responsible for paying back debt, e.g. if one partner creates a lot of debt

Disagreements can prevent quick and effective decision making

Decision making can be slow as **all** partners need to be consulted

Limited liability partnership

Operates in the same way as a traditional partnership. However, the owners are not personally responsible for all of the business's debts. They can only lose the amount of money they originally invested in the business. This is because the business has limited liability.

More paperwork is needed to set up a **limited liability partnership** which can be expensive initially.

Examples: solicitors, accountants

Ownership: two or more owners

Liability: limited

Decision making: split equally between the partners

Profits: split equally between the partners

Revise it!

Look at the advantages and disadvantages of the five forms of ownership and write up to three words in your notes to summarise each advantage and disadvantage.

Remember it!

- Partnerships generally have unlimited liability. Only a limited liability partnership has limited liability.
- Profits are usually divided equally between partners which can lead to disagreements if some partners do more work than others!

Forms of business ownership 3 see p. 95

- Identify appropriate forms of ownership for start-up businesses.
- Analyse the relative advantages and disadvantages of each form of ownership.

Private limited company (Ltd)

A small or medium sized company that is owned by **shareholders**.

Each shareholder invests money into the business and receives a share of the profits (based on the number of shares that they have purchased) in the form of a **dividend**.

Shareholders employ a board of directors to run the business.

Examples: Dyson Ltd, Iceland Ltd, Specsavers Ltd

Ownership: shareholders

Liability: limited

Decision making: board of directors

Profits: dividend paid to shareholders based on the number of shares they each hold

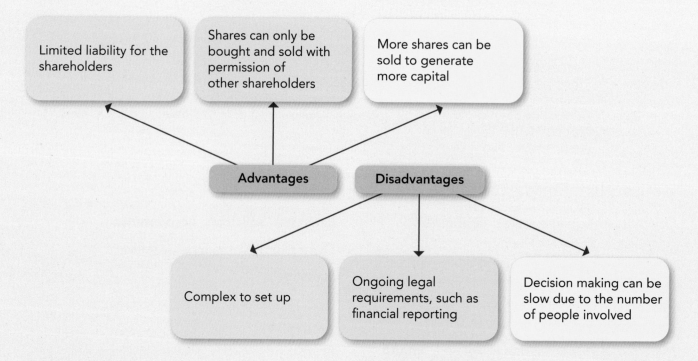

Limited liability for the shareholders

Shares can only be bought and sold with permission of other shareholders

More shares can be sold to generate more capital

Advantages   **Disadvantages**

Complex to set up

Ongoing legal requirements, such as financial reporting

Decision making can be slow due to the number of people involved

Practise it!

1 Other than a sole trader, state *three* different forms of ownership for a business start-up. **(3 marks)**

2 Analyse *two* advantages of setting up a new business as a sole trader. **(6 marks)**

Remember it!

- Private limited companies and limited liability partnerships both benefit from limited liability, so the owners can only lose the amount that they originally invested if the business fails/ goes into debt.
- They cannot be forced to sell their personal possessions to pay for the business's debts.

Forms of business ownership 4 see pp. 93–95

What you need to know

- Identify appropriate forms of ownership for start-up businesses.
- Analyse the relative advantages and disadvantages of each form of ownership.

Franchise

An established business allows entrepreneurs to set up their own business using its brand name, products, training and marketing in return for a **royalty fee**.

The entrepreneur chooses how to 'own' their business (sole trader, partnership, etc.) which trades under the franchisor's business name.

Franchisor: the business that sells the right to operate under its name

Franchisee: the entrepreneur or business that has bought the right to operate under the franchisor's brand.

Examples: Domino's, Spar convenience stores, Anytime Fitness gyms

Ownership: the franchisor owns the brand name. The franchisee owns the right to operate under the brand name

Liability: depends on the entrepreneur's choice of ownership type

Decision making: The franchisor is responsible for key business decisions. The franchisee may be permitted to make decisions about smaller, local matters such as staff, working hours and holidays

Profits: The franchisee earns profit but must pay the franchisor a royalty fee

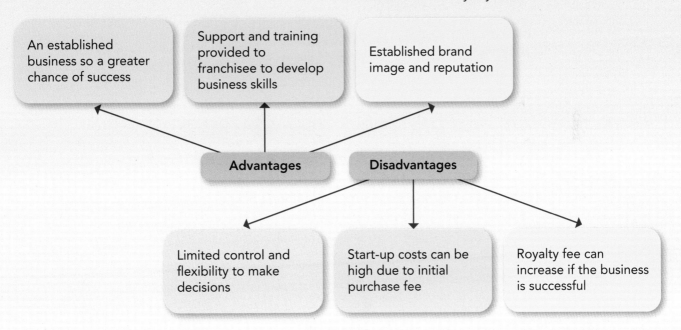

An established business so a greater chance of success

Support and training provided to franchisee to develop business skills

Established brand image and reputation

Advantages   **Disadvantages**

Limited control and flexibility to make decisions

Start-up costs can be high due to initial purchase fee

Royalty fee can increase if the business is successful

Practise it!

Explain *one* advantage and *one* disadvantage of operating as a **franchise**.   **(4 marks)**

Remember it!

- Franchises allow a business to 'buy into' an established business and reduce the risk that the business will fail.
- However, they can be expensive to set up, and the franchisee is limited in their decision making.

Liability  see p. 95

What you need to know

- State the meanings of the terms limited liability and unlimited liability.
- Identify and explain the advantages and disadvantages of limited and unlimited liability.

Liabilities are the legal responsibilities of a business in terms of what it owes, e.g. debt.

Limited liability

Limited liability

The business and owners are separate legal bodies

Any debts owed belong to the business

The owners can only lose up to the amount they have invested

They cannot be forced to sell personal possessions (e.g. a house) to repay debts

Limited liability partnership	Private limited company

Unlimited liability

Unlimited liability

The business and owners are legally responsible for **all** debts

Any debts must be paid using the owners' own money

The owners may have to sell their personal possessions to pay off any debts

Sole trader	Partnership

Practise it!

1   Satnam is thinking of setting up a business with two other people, so any profits would have to be shared between them. The owners have full liability for the debts of the business and may have to sell personal possessions to repay any debt. Which type of business is Satnam thinking of investing in?   **(1 mark)**

    a   **Limited liability** partnership ☐

    b   Partnership ☐

    c   **Private limited company** ☐

    d   Sole trader ☐

2   Identify *two* forms of business ownership with **unlimited liability**.   **(2 marks)**

3   Explain *one* advantage of limited liability for the owner of a business.   **(2 marks)**

Remember it!

- Limited liability limits the owners' responsibility for business debts.
- The owners cannot lose more than the amount that they originally invested in the business.
- They cannot be forced to sell their personal possessions to repay business debts.

Sources of capital 1 see p. 96

What you need to know

- Identify sources of capital available to an entrepreneur for business start-up or expansion.
- Analyse the relative advantages and disadvantages of each source of capital.

Capital is needed when starting up or expanding a business.

Own savings

Personal funds that an entrepreneur has saved up

Money received when made redundant from a job

An **inheritance**

Friends and family

A **gift** or a **loan** from family or friends who might want to invest informally in the business

Loans

Where capital is borrowed from a bank or other financial lender

The amount borrowed is paid back at an agreed rate of interest

Repayments are spread over a set period of time

The term and amounts are determined by the lender

Sources of capital

Business angels

A successful and wealthy entrepreneur who wants to support other entrepreneurs

They provide capital, advice and guidance

Grants

Money given to a business to help with start-up and expansion

Generally the funds do not have to be repaid

Crowdfunding

Raising money by asking different people to invest in return for a small share of the business

Usually done online through a crowdfunding website

Revise it!

Write the name of each source of capital in the centre of a blank sheet of paper.

Create a mind map using the spider diagram on this page. Add the advantages and disadvantages of each source of capital (see Sources of capital 2).

Use a different-colour pen to show which ones are advantages and which ones are disadvantages.

Put the mind map on your wall to support your revision.

Remember it!

- There is no formal agreement to pay the money back when using own savings.
- The arrangements regarding a gift or loan from friends or family are also often informal.
- However, the other sources of capital generally involve formal arrangements/ contracts with conditions attached.

Sources of capital 2 see p. 96

What you need to know

- Assess the advantages and disadvantages of the different sources of capital.

Entrepreneurs must consider the advantages and disadvantages of each source of capital to help them choose the most appropriate one to use.

Source of funding	Advantages	Disadvantages
Own savings	No requirement to pay back the investment No bank fees, interest or application fees	The amount available is limited to the value of savings held by the entrepreneur Savings are tied up so they cannot be used for other purchases or emergencies
Friends and family	Can be an informal arrangement with no formal repayments No bank fees or application fees	May cause tension if the money cannot be repaid They might try to interfere with the running of the business, leading to disagreements Amount of capital available is limited to what friends/family have
Loans	The lender will not ask for the loan to be repaid at short notice Repayments are set at a fixed amount each month, which helps the entrepreneur to budget	Entrepreneur pays back more than they borrow because interest is charged Lender may ask for assets as security in case the entrepreneur cannot repay the loan
Crowdfunding	Can raise large amounts of capital Raises the profile of the business before the product is launched More suitable for riskier business ventures	Can take a while to raise the required investment No guarantee that it will raise the full amount of capital Investors may want a share of the profit and might interfere with how the business is run
Grants	Many grants are available No interest is charged on grants and often they do not need to be repaid	Usually have conditions, so the business may not be eligible Application process is detailed and time-consuming
Business angels	Can share relevant experience, offer advice and useful contacts May be able to invest a large amount of money	Might ask for a share of the profits or part ownership of the business Might interfere with business decisions

Practise it!

1. State *one* disadvantage of crowdfunding. **(1 mark)**
2. Analyse *one* advantage of the entrepreneur using their own savings as a source of capital. **(3 marks)**

Remember it!

There are many sources of capital available to entrepreneurs. It is important to analyse the advantages and disadvantages of the different sources to choose the most appropriate one(s) for the type of business and the purpose it will be used for.

Support for enterprise see pp. 97–98

What you need to know

- Explain the different sources of support available to entrepreneurs.
- Analyse the relative advantages and limitations of the types of support.

Entrepreneurs are likely to need support when setting up and running a business. This may be financial or legal support, information, or training and advice to develop business skills. There are many sources of support, which can be seen here:

Finance providers

Banks often provide free advice to support an entrepreneur to make good decisions

Business angels can share experience and contacts with the entrepreneur

Charities

Often provide free support focusing on investment or training to develop skills (e.g. The Prince's Trust provides mentors, training, and advice and guidance)

Support may be limited if the charity lacks funding

Solicitors

Provide legal advice, deal with legal matters and ensure that the business is abiding by the law

Solicitors specialise in different areas, e.g. tax solicitors specialise in issues related to the tax system

Usually they charge a fee, which can be expensive

Accountants

They can support entrepreneurs by preparing their accounts and tax returns and by providing financial advice

Services can be expensive

They can help to organise the business so that its finances work effectively and it makes good financial decisions

Friends/family

Informal business advice and moral support based on their own experiences

Friends/family may not be up to date with current requirements

Local council enterprise department

Encourages new businesses/business expansion

It can support entrepreneurs by providing: free or low-cost advice and information; local data and statistics; grants; and training sessions.

Government

The government supports businesses because successful businesses contribute to the economy

They provide information, capital, training and support (e.g. mentoring schemes and support helplines)

Can be time-consuming finding relevant information

Chamber of Commerce

A network of local business owners/entrepreneurs that meets regularly and promotes the interests of local businesses

It provides opportunities to meet other local business owners and build useful contacts to help with growing the business

Practise it!

1   Albi is looking for advice regarding a contract with a supplier. Identify a suitable source of support.   **(1 mark)**

2   Explain *two* advantages of asking a family member for advice when setting up a new business.   **(4 marks)**

Remember it!

- There are many sources of support available to entrepreneurs.
- An entrepreneur should decide on the most appropriate source based on their needs.

Characteristics, risk and reward for enterprise see pp. 19–21

1   Which one of these is *not* a characteristic of being a successful entrepreneur?
    Circle (◯) the correct answer.   **(1 mark)**

    (a) Risk-taking   **(b)** Creativity

    (c) Recklessness   **(d)** Negotiation

2   Stephanie is hoping to set up a small catering business. She completed a
    business course at school and remembers that successful entrepreneurs
    share certain characteristics. Explain *two* characteristics of being a
    successful entrepreneur.
    One has been started for you.   **(4 marks)**

    Characteristic 1   *Determination*
    ....

    Explanation   *An entrepreneur will need to be determined because*
    ....

    ....

    Characteristic 2 ....

    Explanation ....

    ....

3   Explain why an entrepreneur's work–life balance may be negatively affected
    when taking a risk to start up a new business.   **(2 marks)**

    Explanation ....

    ....

4   Entrepreneurs have to take risks when setting up a new business. There are many
    potential drawbacks of risk-taking but there are many potential rewards.
    Explain *two* potential rewards of taking a risk.   **(4 marks)**

    Explanation 1..

    ....

    ....

    Explanation 2..

    ....

    ....

Market research 1 `see pp. 22–23`

1   Dexi is planning a new business and obtained some profit figures that were published by a competitor. Which *one* of the following is the best definition of the type of market research used by Dexi? Circle (◯) the correct answer.   **(1 mark)**

   (a) Internal   **(b)** Qualitative   **(c)** Primary   **(d)** Secondary

2   State *two* reasons for conducting market research for a new business.   **(2 marks)**

   Reason 1 ....

   Reason 2 ....

3   State *one* benefit of primary market research.   **(1 mark)**

   ....

   ....

4   Which of the following market research sources involves using data which is already held by the business? Tick (✓) the correct answer.   **(1 mark)**

   (a) Competitor data ☐   **(b)** Internal data ☐

   (c) Newspapers ☐   **(d)** Trade magazines ☐

5   Rani is planning a new childcare nursery in her local town and would like to carry out some market research to understand the market and estimate the likely demand for her services. She has downloaded some government statistics about the population in the town. Analyse *two* advantages of Rani using government statistics as part of her market research.   **(6 marks)**

   Advantage 1 ....

   ....

   ....

   Advantage 2 ....

   ....

   ....

6   Identify *two* other secondary market research sources that Rani could use.   **(2 marks)**

   1 ....

   2 ....

Market research 2 see p. 24

1   Explain *one* advantage and *one* disadvantage of carrying out your market research using newspapers, trade magazines and/or books.   **(4 marks)**

Advantage ....

Explanation ....

....

....

....

Disadvantage ....

Explanation ....

....

....

....

2   Louis is planning to set up a small shop and would like to carry out market research to find out his customers' preferences regarding the opening times.

Analyse *one* advantage and *one* disadvantage of conducting primary market research. One has been started for you.   **(6 marks)**

Advantage   *One advantage of conducting primary market research is that it is tailored to Louis' business idea.*

Explanation   *Louis can design the questions so that he gets the information he needs. The impact of this on the business is*

....

....

....

Disadvantage ....

Explanation ....

....

....

Workbook

Quantitative and qualitative data see p. 27

1 Define the terms 'quantitative data' and 'qualitative data'. **(4 marks)**

   Quantitative data: ....

   ....

   ....

   Qualitative data: ....

   ....

   ....

2 Identify *two* secondary market research sources that may present
   quantitative data. **(2 marks)**

   1 ....

   2 ....

3 Explain *one* advantage of quantitative data. **(2 marks)**

   ....

   ....

4 Sasha has run a focus group with *six* customers which has collected qualitative data.

   Explain *one* advantage and *one* limitation of using qualitative data. **(4 marks)**

   Advantage ....

   Explanation ....

   ....

   ....

   ....

   Limitation ....

   Explanation ....

   ....

   ....

Types of market segmentation and their benefits see pp. 28–29

1 What is market segmentation? Circle (○) the correct answer.   **(1 mark)**

   (a) A method of advertising a new product

   (b) A way of finding out customer views on a new product idea

   (c) Dividing a market by lifestyle, gender, age, etc.

   (d) A secondary market research source

2 Dividing a group of customers by how much they earn is an example of which type of market segmentation? Circle (○) the correct answer.   **(1 mark)**

   (a) Age   **(b)** Lifestyle   **(c)** Hair colour   **(d)** Gender   **(e)** Income

3 Which *one* of the following is a reason why businesses segment the market? Circle (○) the correct answer.   **(1 mark)**

   (a) To aid in decision making   **(c)** It is a legal requirement

   (b) To develop a brand image   **(d)** To meet different customers' needs

4 You have started a business making jigsaw puzzles. You will offer two ranges of jigsaw puzzle – one will feature characters from popular children's television programmes and the other will feature local landmarks.

   (a) Identify *two* types of market segmentation that you could use.   **(2 marks)**

   1 ....

   2 ....

   (b) Explain *two* benefits of market segmentation in increasing the profitability of the business.   **(4 marks)**

   > **Tip:** Think about: age (type of image, number of pieces), gender (type of image), location (image of a local landmark), etc.

   Benefit 1 ....

   Explanation ....

   ....

   Benefit 2 ....

   Explanation ....

   ....

Fixed, variable and total costs 1 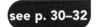 see p. 30–32

1 Explain, using an example, what is meant by **variable costs**. **(3 marks)**

....

....

....

2 Wages are an example of what? Tick (✓) the correct answer. **(1 mark)**

(a) Fixed costs ☐ **(b)** Revenue ☐ **(c)** Total costs ☐ **(d)** Variable costs ☐

3 Harpreet runs a business making wooden furniture. She has a small factory which she rents. She has a loan which she took out to expand the business. She has one part-time employee and is advertising for a second part-time employee. Harpreet delivers all of the furniture directly to customers' homes and packages all of the products carefully to ensure the items reach customers safely.

Identify *three* fixed costs and *three* variable costs of Harpreet's business. **(6 marks)**

Fixed costs:

1 ....

2 ....

3 ....

Variable costs:

1 ....

2 ....

3 ....

4 Iris runs a small taxi business and has calculated the following costs during an average month:

- Fixed costs: £3000
- Total costs: £4500

(a) Calculate the variable costs per month for Iris's business. Show your workings. **(1 mark)**

(b) Calculate the fixed costs per year for Iris's business. Show your workings. **(1 mark)**

Fixed, variable and total costs 2 see pp. 30–32

Mary has opened a business selling takeaway cakes. She has the following costs:

- Rent: £300 per month.
- Utilities: £50 per month.
- Ingredients: £2.30 per cake slice.

- Packaging: £0.50 per cake slice.
- Salaries: £600 per month.

She predicts that she will sell 1350 slices of cake per month.

1 Calculate Mary's total fixed costs per month. Show your workings. **(1 mark)**

> **Tip:** Mary's fixed costs are the costs that do not change if the number of cakes made changes.

2 Calculate Mary's total variable costs per month based on her meeting her sales target. Show your workings. **(3 marks)**

3 Calculate Mary's total costs per year if she sells an average of 1350 slices of cake per month. Remember there are 12 months in a year. Show your workings. **(2 marks)**

4 Mary over-estimated her sales figures. In an average month, she sold 950 slices of cake. Calculate her total costs per month based on her actual sales figures. Show your workings. **(4 marks)**

Revenue generated by sales see p. 33

1 Which *one* of the following is the formula to calculate the revenue made by a business? Tick (✓) the correct answer. **(1 mark)**

    (a) Selling price per unit + number of sales ☐

    (b) Selling price per unit − number of sales ☐

    (c) Selling price per unit ÷ number of sales ☐

    (d) Selling price per unit × number of sales ☐

2 Explain what is meant by total revenue. **(2 marks)**

> **Tip:** In the exam, the term 'revenue' could be used on its own.

....

....

3 Sunita is setting up a small business selling party bags for children's parties. She intends to sell two types of party bags:

- Luxury party bags: £5.99
- Standard party bags: £3.50

Sunita estimates that in an average week she will sell 30 luxury party bags and 55 standard party bags.

    (a) Calculate the total revenue she expects to make in an average week. Show your workings. **(3 marks)**

    (b) Assuming that sales are the same each week, calculate how much revenue Sunita will generate for the whole year. Show your workings. **(2 marks)**

> **Tip:** Don't forget, there are 52 weeks in a year!

Sunita's raw materials are more costly than she realised. She has had to increase her selling price and has decided to sell only the standard party bag.
Her standard party bag is now £4.99. Sunita estimates that in an average week she will sell 48 standard party bags.

(c) Calculate the total revenue she expects to make in a four-week period.
Show your workings. **(2 marks)**

4   Pavel runs a small business selling personalised gifts.

(a) Last week Pavel earned £6000 of revenue. The average gift price last week was £25.
How many gifts did he sell? Circle (O) the correct answer. **(1 mark)**

> **Tip:** For this question you will need to rearrange the total revenue formula:
> selling price per unit × number of sales

   i   500
   ii   240
   iii 150
   iv   32

(b) Pavel generated £1350 of revenue last month. He sold 25 items.
Calculate his average selling price. Show your workings. **(2 marks)**

> **Tip:** Remember the formula to find the average selling price:
> total revenue ÷ number of sales

Profit and loss see p. 34

1   A business earns £21 000 of revenue. Its total costs are £6000.

How much profit does the business make? Circle (○) the correct answer.   **(1 mark)**

(a) £14 500   (b) £5000   (c) £27 000   (d) £15 000

2   Adil runs a dry-cleaning business. In April he earned £9620 in revenue.
His total costs for the month were £11 423.
Which *one* of the following best describes the situation Adil's business is in?
Circle (○) the correct answer.   **(1 mark)**

(a) Cash flow   (b) Loss   (c) Profit   (d) Break-even

3   Dawn has calculated her costs per week to be:

- Rent £150
- Utilities £25
- Raw materials £450
- Salaries £200

She forecasts that her average revenue per month will be £13 500.
There are four weeks in a month.

(a) Calculate Dawn's total costs per month. Show your workings.   **(2 marks)**

> **Tip:** Make sure you read the question carefully, especially the time period
> for costs and revenue as you may need to convert some of the figures to
> a consistent time period!

(b) Calculate Dawn's profit per month. Show your workings.   **(2 marks)**

(c) Two months later Dawn makes £20 500 profit. Assuming her total costs
remained the same, calculate the revenue Dawn made that month.   **(3 marks)**

> **Tip:** For this question you will need to rearrange the profit/loss formula.

Break-even see p. 36

$$\text{break-even quantity (in units)} = \frac{\text{fixed costs}}{\text{selling price per unit} - \text{variable cost per unit}}$$

Tip: Often the answers from break-even calculations need to be 'rounded up' to the next whole number as an entrepreneur cannot generally sell a portion of a product to a customer.

1   In March, Claire's business has fixed costs of £225. Her variable costs are £23 per unit and she sells her product at £40 per item.

Using the formula above, calculate her break-even point in March.
Show your workings.   **(2 marks)**

2   Claire has recently found out that her fixed costs are going to increase. In April they will be £310. Her variable costs and the price of the product will remain the same.

Using the formula above, calculate how many more products Claire will have to sell in April to break even. Show your workings.   **(3 marks)**

3 Claire introduces a new product. She needs to sell 20 products to break even each month. The fixed costs for the new product total £1260 per month and the variable costs per unit total £30.

Calculate the selling price of the new product. Show your workings. **(4 marks)**

> **Tip:** To calculate the selling price you will need to rearrange the break-even formula.

4 State *one* consequence of Claire's business not breaking even. **(1 mark)**

....

....

5 State *three* things that a business will be unable to do if it does not have enough cash. **(3 marks)**

1 ....

2 ....

3 ....

Interpreting a break-even graph see p. 37

A break-even graph for Lily's business is shown below.

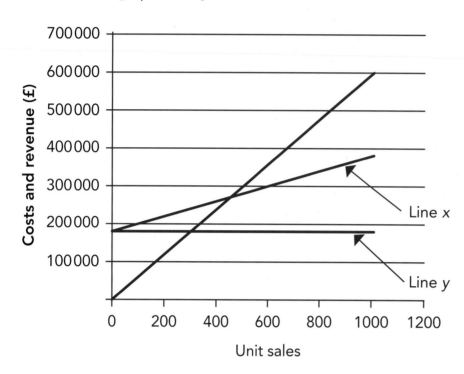

1   What does line *x* represent? Circle (○) the correct answer.   **(1 mark)**

(a) Fixed costs

(b) Total costs

(c) Sales revenue

(d) Break-even point

2   What does line *y* represent? Circle (○) the correct answer.   **(1 mark)**

(a) Fixed costs

(b) Total costs

(c) Sales revenue

(d) Break-even point

3   Using the graph, find out the total revenue for sales of 800 units.   **(1 mark)**

....

4   Using the graph, state whether the business will make a profit or a loss if it
    sells 200 units.   **(1 mark)**

....

5 Using the graph, state whether the business will make a profit or a loss if it sells 800 units. **(1 mark)**

....

6 Which of the following decisions might break-even information support? Circle (◯) the correct answer. **(1 mark)**

(a) Where to sell a new product

(b) Whether to carry out additional market research

(c) Where to advertise a new product

(d) What price to charge

The importance of cash see pp. 38–39

1 State *two* reasons why a business needs to maintain enough cash. **(2 marks)**

1 ....

2 ....

2 Explain *three* possible reasons why a business may be short of cash despite being profitable. **(6 marks)**

....

....

....

....

....

....

The marketing mix see p. 40

1 Which of the following is *not* one of the elements of the marketing mix?
   Circle (◯) the correct answer. **(1 mark)**

   (a) Packaging

   (b) Place

   (c) Product

   (d) Promotion

2 State which *one* element of the marketing mix affects whether a customer
  will be able to afford the product. **(1 mark)**

   ....

3 Karlton runs a business that sells sportswear to professional football clubs.
  He currently sells a high-quality football jersey in specialist sports retailers who
  promote it in publications aimed at professional sports players. The product
  is priced 25 percent lower than similar products sold by competitors. Karlton's
  business is not very profitable and his bank manager has suggested that he
  reviews his marketing mix. Customers are wary of buying his products
  because of the low price.

  Analyse why decisions regarding price and product should be aligned
  with those for other elements of the marketing mix. **(6 marks)**

   ....

   ....

   ....

   ....

   ....

   ....

   ....

   ....

   ....

   ....

   ....

Workbook

Digital and non-digital advertising mediums 1 see pp. 41, 44

1 Read the descriptions of types of advertising. Decide if each one is an example of a digital or non-digital advertising medium. Draw lines to match. **(6 marks)**

Type of advertising medium

Description

A radio advert to promote a prize competition

A social media feed to launch a new product

Non-digital advertising medium

A billboard advertising a new product

A specialist magazine advertising a 10 percent discount

Digital advertising medium

A leaflet to promote a new product

A promotional text message sent to clients

2   Marcin has recently set up a new business selling customised jewellery.
    Identify *two* digital advertising methods that he could use to attract customers
    to his new business.   **(2 marks)**

    1   ....

    2   ....

3   Analyse *two* benefits of advertising on the radio. One has been started for you.   **(6 marks)**

    Benefit 1   *Radio stations are often targeted at specific segments of the market.*

    > **Tip:** Think about how targeting a specific market segment may help the business.

    Explanation ....

    ....

    ....

    Benefit 2 ....

    Explanation ....

    ....

    ....

Digital and non-digital advertising mediums 2 see pp. 42, 45

1 You are an entrepreneur and have recently decided to work with a business angel to launch a new vegan café in your local town. You will sell a range of vegan foods and drinks. You have found a café on the town's high street close to an industrial estate that has a wide range of offices and factories. You intend to offer a takeaway ordering service at lunchtime.

(a) Analyse *two* disadvantages of using non-digital billboards as a method of advertising. One has been started for you. **(6 marks)**

Disadvantage 1 *One drawback of using a billboard as a method of advertising is that the best (most prominent) locations to advertise in are very expensive. This might be a problem for a small business because*

....

The impact on the business would be

....

Disadvantage 2 ....

....

....

....

....

(b) Identify *two* other non-digital advertising mediums that the business could consider.

(2 marks)

1 ....

2 ....

2 You are planning a new plumbing business and you want to advertise to make people in your local town aware of your services. You are considering whether to use either leaflets or social media to advertise your new business. Discuss the advantages and disadvantages of the two methods and decide which one you will use. Justify your decision. Your recommendation should include:

- an advantage and a disadvantage of using leaflets
- an advantage and a disadvantage of using social media
- your choice of either leaflets or social media
- a justification for your decision. **(8 marks)**

....

....

....

....

....

....

....

....

....

....

....

....

....

....

....

....

Sales promotion techniques and public relations `see pp. 47–50`

1. A coffee shop buys equipment for the local football club in return for having its logo on the players' shirts.
   What is this type of sales promotion called? Circle (◯) the correct answer. **(1 mark)**

   (a) Product trial

   (b) Competition

   (c) Loyalty scheme

   (d) Sponsorship

2. Which *one* of the following sales promotion techniques rewards customers for their repeat business over a period of time? Circle (◯) the correct answer. **(1 mark)**

   (a) Competitions

   (b) Loyalty schemes

   (c) Discounts

   (d) Buy one get one free

3. Analyse *one* benefit and *one* limitation of running a prize competition as a sales promotion technique to attract customers. One has been started for you. **(6 marks)**

   Tip: How might the additional publicity benefit the business?

   Benefit *An exciting prize may generate a lot of additional publicity, e.g. word of mouth or social media sharing by excited customers.*

   Limitation ....

   ....

   ....

   ....

4. Using famous people to promote a brand is an example of what?
   Tick (✓) the correct answer. **(1 mark)**

   (a) Product placement ☐   (b) Press release ☐

   (c) Sponsorship ☐   (d) Celebrity endorsement ☐

How to sell goods and services see p. 51

1 Mo wants his customers to be able to touch his product and try it out.
State the best method for Mo to sell his product. **(1 mark)**

....

2 State *two* digital ways of selling goods and services. **(2 marks)**

1 ....

2 ....

3 Explain *one* advantage and *one* disadvantage of selling goods and services
through social media. One has been started for you. **(4 marks)**

Advantage *The customer can purchase at their own convenience.*

Explanation *Social media is available* .... *so customers can*

....

Disadvantage ....

Explanation ....

....

4 Explain *two* reasons why a high-end furniture retailer would choose to sell its
products in a shop rather than online. **(4 marks)**

1 ....

....

2 ....

....

5   Narinder has set up a business making samosas. He needs to decide whether to sell them face to face at the local market or digitally. He is not making enough samosas to sell them through both physical and digital channels.

Discuss the advantages and disadvantages of the two ways of selling to customers and decide which one Narinder should use. Justify your decision. Your recommendation should include:

- an advantage and a disadvantage of physical channels
- an advantage and a disadvantage of digital channels
- your choice of either physical or digital channels
- a justification for your decision.   (8 marks)

....

....

....

....

....

....

....

....

....

....

....

....

....

....

....

....

....

The product lifecycle and extension strategies see p. 52–55

1 Which of the following is *not* a stage of the product lifecycle?
Circle (○) the correct answer. **(1 mark)**

   (a) Development

   (b) Boom

   (c) Introduction

   (d) Growth

2 Narinder makes and sells samosas. He carried out market research and improved the recipe using customer feedback.

   (a) Label the stages of the product lifecycle that Narinder's samosas will go through on the diagram below. The first one has been labelled for you. **(5 marks)**

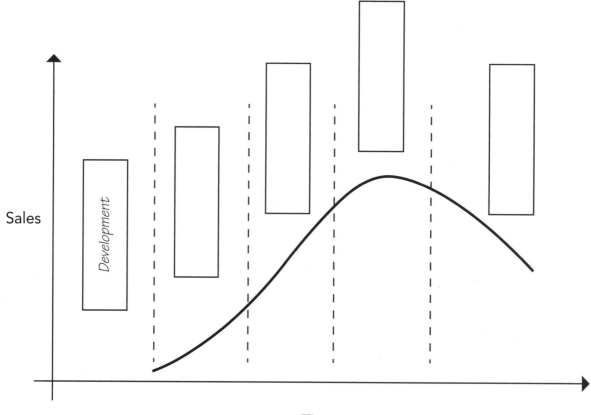

   (b) Narinder launched his samosas onto the market so that customers could try them. Customers have now become aware of his product and sales have increased rapidly. Identify which stage of the product lifecycle Narinder's product is in. **(1 mark)**

   ....

(c) Explain *one* decision that the product lifecycle may help Narinder to make. **(2 marks)**

Decision ....

Explanation ....

....

(d) Explain *two* extension strategies that Narinder could use to improve sales of his samosas in the future. **(4 marks)**

Strategy 1 ....

Explanation ....

....

Strategy 2 ....

Explanation ....

....

Pricing 1 see p. 57

1   Which pricing strategy starts with a high price that reduces over time?
    Circle (○) the correct answer.   **(1 mark)**

    (a) Competitive pricing

    (b) Price skimming

    (c) Psychological pricing

    (d) Price penetration

2   **(a)** Which *one* of the following pricing strategies is an example of
    price penetration? Tick (✓) the correct answer.   **(1 mark)**

    Keeping the price of the product high to make it exclusive.   ☐

    Setting a low price at the start to encourage people to purchase,   ☐
    then increasing the price after the introductory period.

    Ending the price with 99p to make it appear to be a bargain.   ☐

    Keeping the price in line with the price of competitors' goods.   ☐

    (b) Explain *one* advantage and *one* disadvantage of price penetration.   **(4 marks)**

    Advantage...

    Explanation ....

    ....

    Disadvantage ....

    Explanation ....

    ....

3   You plan to sell a new range of personalised pens at £12.99.
    Identify what this pricing strategy is called.   **(1 mark)**

    ....

4   Ben and Aleesha are considering using competitive pricing for their new greetings cards.
    Explain what is meant by competitive pricing.   **(2 marks)**

    ....

    ....

    ....

    ....

5 Explain *two* factors that an entrepreneur should consider when setting the price of the product. One has been started for you. **(4 marks)**

Factor 1 *Income of the target audience.*

Explanation *An entrepreneur needs to know how much the target audience earns so that they can set the price of the product at an amount that the target audience*

Factor 2

Explanation

Pricing 2 see p. 57

1   You have launched a new business selling vegan ready-meals. The meals are sold online via your business website and you deliver them straight to the customer's home. Discuss whether you should use **competitive pricing** or **psychological pricing** to advertise your business. Then choose one and justify your answer.
    Include:

    • an advantage and a disadvantage of using competitive pricing
    • an advantage and a disadvantage of using psychological pricing
    • a justification for your decision.   (8 marks)

    ....
    ....
    ....
    ....
    ....
    ....
    ....
    ....
    ....
    ....
    ....
    ....
    ....
    ....
    ....
    ....
    ....
    ....

Workbook

Forms of business ownership and liability 1 see pp. 58, 62

1   You run a business as a sole trader.

(a) Explain what is meant by sole trader. **(2 marks)**

....

....

....

(b) Identify *two* other types of business ownership that you could have considered
for your business. **(2 marks)**

1 ....

2 ....

(c) Explain *one* advantage of operating as a sole trader. **(2 marks)**

....

....

....

2   Which *one* of the following is an advantage of running a business as a partnership?
Circle (○) the correct answer. **(1 mark)**

(a) The profit must be shared amongst the partners.

(b) Unlimited liability.

(c) The workload and decision making can be shared.

(d) It may take longer to make decisions.

3   You are considering setting up your own café focusing on vegan food. You are
going to work with your friend Paul and you have to decide on the type of ownership.
Paul would like the business to be a partnership.
Analyse *two* disadvantages of operating as a partnership. **(6 marks)**

Disadvantage 1 ....

....

....

....

Disadvantage 2 ....

....

....

....

4 What is the correct name for a business that purchases the rights to operate under the name of an existing business? Circle (◯) the correct answer.　　**(1 mark)**

　　(a) A sole trader

　　(b) A franchisee

　　(c) A partner

　　(d) A franchisor

Forms of business ownership and liability 2 see pp. 59, 62

1   As a sole trader you have unlimited liability.
    What does 'unlimited liability' mean? Circle (○) the correct answer.   **(1 mark)**

    (a) You are at risk of losing your personal possessions if the business goes into debt.

    (b) You are only liable for the money you put into the business.

    (c) You can keep all the profit that the business makes.

    (d) You share responsibility for the business risk with the other owners.

2   Which *one* of the following is a disadvantage of unlimited liability for the
    owners of a business? Circle (○) the correct answer.   **(1 mark)**

    (a) The owners can only lose the amount that they invested in the business if it fails.

    (b) The owners must share the profit between them.

    (c) The owners may have to sell their personal possessions to repay business debts.

    (d) The owners have more freedom for decision making.

3   Identify *two* types of business ownership that have unlimited liability.   **(2 marks)**

    1 ....

    2 ....

4   Identify *two* types of business ownership that have limited liability.   **(2 marks)**

    1 ....

    2 ....

Sources of capital (see pp. 63–64)

1   Which *one* of the following sources of capital for a business often has strict conditions attached but does not usually have to be paid back?
Circle (○) the correct answer. **(1 mark)**

    (a) Loan   **(b)** Grant   **(c)** Crowdfunding   **(d)** Own savings

2   A partnership takes a loan to help to expand the business.
Which one of the following *best* describes this source of capital?
Circle (○) the correct answer. **(1 mark)**

    (a) Capital provided by a bank with a formal repayment schedule that includes interest

    (b) A gift from a relative

    (c) Capital provided by a charity that has strict conditions attached but does not have to be repaid

    (d) The partners' own savings

3   Explain what a business angel is. **(2 marks)**

....

....

....

4   Zoe has recently left her job at a local hair salon and has decided to open her own salon as a sole trader. Her family have offered to give her some of the capital to set up the business.

    (a) Identify *two* other sources of capital that Zoe could use to start up her business. **(2 marks)**

       1 ....

       2 ....

    (b) Explain *one* advantage and *one* disadvantage of using money from friends and family as a source of capital. **(4 marks)**

....

....

....

....

....

....

Support for enterprise see p. 65

1   A start-up business needs some advice but they do not want to have to pay for it.
    Which one of the following sources of support should they avoid?
    Circle (◯) the correct answer.   **(1 mark)**

    (a) Chamber of Commerce

    (b) Accountant

    (c) Friends and family

    (d) Government

2   A partnership needs legal advice about bringing a new partner into the business.
    Which one of the following would be the *best* form of support?
    Circle (◯) the correct answer.   **(1 mark)**

    (a) Solicitor

    (b) Charities

    (c) Friends and family

    (d) Local government/council

3   Identify *two* ways, other than providing capital, that a bank or business angel
    can support an entrepreneur.   **(2 marks)**

    1 ....

    2 ....

4   Explain *one* way a charity could support an entrepreneur.   **(2 marks)**

    ....

    ....

    ....

    ....

5   Lyle runs a successful wedding planning business. He has applied to join his
    local Chamber of Commerce.
    Explain *two* advantages to Lyle's business of joining the Chamber
    of Commerce.   **(4 marks)**

....

....

....

....

....

....

....

....

Glossary

Key terms

Accountant: A professional who prepares and analyses financial records and accounts.

Advertising: A promotion technique to inform and attract customers to buy a specific product.

Biased: A tendency to favour one thing or person over another.

Convenience sampling reduces possible bias in the findings because it does not target specific groups.

Break-even point: The point at which a business is not making a profit or a loss. The total costs are equal to the total revenue generated.

Break-even quantity: The number of units that the business needs to sell to break even.

Business angel: An experienced business owner who offers capital to support entrepreneurs to start or expand a business.

Capital: A sum of money owned by a business or used in a business for start-up or one-off expansion/investment.

The entrepreneur used their own savings to invest capital into their new business.

Cash: The physical money (notes and coins) that a business holds within the business and its bank account so that it is readily available to pay any debts or expenses.

The business had enough cash to pay all of its bills.

Celebrity endorsement: Using a celebrity's popularity or social status to sell a brand.

Chamber of Commerce: An organisation that promotes the interests of local business owners and entrepreneurs within a local area.

Charity: A not-for-profit organisation that raises money to support a specific cause.

Competitive pricing: A pricing strategy where prices are set in line with competitors' prices.

Competitors: Other businesses that offer goods and services similar to those offered by the entrepreneur's business. The other business will try to meet the needs and wants of the same customers as those that the entrepreneur is targeting.

Components: Parts that are used to produce a product.

Costs: The money that a business has to pay out to run the business. That is, the expenses that a business incurs to produce and sell its goods and services.

Crowdfunding: A way of raising capital from a large number of people who each contribute a portion of the amount required. Usually the money is generated by advertising the business idea on a crowdfunding website to attract 'sponsors' to offer money.

Customer profile: The main characteristics of a customer or group of customers.

Data: Facts and figures that have been collected through research.

Dividend: A share of the profits that a company pays out to its shareholders.

E-commerce: This stands for electronic commerce and it is the buying and selling of goods and services over the internet.

Entrepreneur: An individual who sets up a new business providing a good or service that people are willing to buy to satisfy their needs. The entrepreneur bears the risk and receives the rewards of the business.

Extension strategy: A strategy used by an entrepreneur to stimulate more sales of a product when it is reaching the end of the product lifecycle.

Facilitator: A person who coordinates a focus group by asking questions and directing the conversation.

Financially viable: Able to generate enough income to cover the costs incurred to run the business.

The business was financially viable because its revenue covered its costs and it made a profit.

Fixed costs: Costs that do not change regardless of the level of output of the business.

The business's fixed costs included rent, electricity and gas bills, and advertising, and they were not affected when the level of output reduced.

Focus group: A group of people that meet to discuss their views on specific products or topics.

The focus group met face to face to discuss their opinions and views on a new range of biscuits.

Franchise: An arrangement where one business allows another business to operate under its brand name or business format, usually in return for a fee.

Many fast-food restaurants, such as Subway and Burger King, operate as franchise businesses whereby the owner of the original business sells the right to operate under a well-known brand.

Franchisee: The business that has bought the right to operate under the franchise's brand name.

The franchisee paid Subway a fee to operate their business under the Subway brand.

Franchisor: The business that owns the franchise and grants a licence to the franchisee to use the brand/business format. Subway is an example of a franchisor that allows other businesses/entrepreneurs to open and run a business using the Subway brand name in return for a fee.

Grants: Capital given to the business by the government or charities to start up or expand a business. Grants do not usually have to repaid.

Inheritance: A sum of money or an object/property that a person is left (bequeathed) when a close friend or relative dies.

Insurance: Insurance offers protection to the entrepreneur against a potential financial loss. The insurance provider guarantees to provide the entrepreneur with financial compensation/payment in the event that an insured event, such as a fire or flood, occurs which causes the entrepreneur to suffer financial loss.

Level of output: The number of units/products produced by a business.

Liability: Being responsible for something, such as paying a debt. The liability may arise as a result of signing a contract or it may be a legal responsibility, such as ensuring safe working conditions for employees.

Limited liability: If the business fails or gets into debt, the owner of the business can only lose the amount that they originally invested. They cannot be forced to sell their personal possessions to pay for the business's debts.

The shareholders of the private limited company lost the amount of money they had invested in shares, but they were not responsible for all of the debts of the business because it had limited liability.

Limited liability partnership: A business that is jointly owned and controlled by two or more people who benefit from limited liability. (*See* **limited liability**)

Loan interest: Money that is paid to a lender for borrowing capital. Interest is how the lender makes money out of lending capital. Interest is usually charged daily and calculated as a percentage of the outstanding sum of money (the balance).

Loss: The amount of money that a business/entrepreneur loses. It is the opposite of a profit.

The business suffered a loss because its total revenue was less than the money it had spent (e.g. costs).

Market segmentation: The process of dividing up a market for a specific product into different groups, or segments, according to different characteristics, such as age, gender, occupation and lifestyle. This allows a business to target relevant customers.

Market share: The proportion of the total sales in a market made by a specific product or business. Market share is often expressed as a percentage.

The toy company increased market share by gaining sales from its competitors.

Marketing mix: The marketing mix is the four elements that the entrepreneur must use to promote their business or product. The four elements are: product, place, promotion and price.

Partnership: A business that is jointly owned and controlled by two or more people. The partners generally have unlimited liability.

Partnership agreement: A contract prepared by the partners when they set up a business as a partnership. The contract will outline how profits/losses are to be shared, the amount of capital invested by each partner, information about how the partnership operates and the role of each partner. A partnership agreement is also known as a deed of partnership.

Podcast: A recording of someone discussing a specific product, business or topic on the internet. Podcasts can be downloaded as audio files.

Press/media release: A summary of a news story that is sent to journalists or radio and TV stations in the hope that they will publish or cover the story, which will generate free publicity for a business.

Price penetration: A pricing strategy in which products are launched with a low price. This price will increase over time as sales increase.

Price skimming: A pricing strategy that involves products being launched with a high price. This price will then reduce over time.

Pricing strategy: The method that businesses use to set a selling price for a product or service.

Primary market research: Data that is collected first-hand, i.e. the researcher collects the data themselves rather than relying on data that has been collected from previous research.

Private limited company: A business that is owned by shareholders. Each shareholder receives a proportion of the profits that the company makes based on the number of shares that the shareholder purchased.

Product lifecycle: A model which shows the stages that a product goes through from when it was created to when it is withdrawn from the market.

Profit: The amount of money that a business or entrepreneur makes. It is calculated by subtracting the money it has spent (e.g. costs to produce a product and operate the business) from its total income.

After a year of trading, Josh had sold enough T-shirts to cover his costs and make a profit.

Promotion: Activities and methods that businesses carry out to make potential customers aware of products and services.

Psychological pricing: A pricing strategy to make products appear cheaper and more affordable by avoiding round numbers, e.g. £9.99 rather than £10.00.

Public relations: Promoting the company's reputation and building a beneficial relationship/positive image between a business and the public.

Qualitative data: Data expressed as opinions and views.

The qualitative data detailed what customers liked about the new baked beans they had bought.

Quantitative data: Data expressed as numbers or facts.

The quantitative data showed the number of people who bought a can of baked beans last week.

Raw materials: The materials, ingredients and resources used to produce a product.

Revenue: The money that a business receives from selling its goods or services.

Josh made £1500 in revenue from selling 100 T-shirts at £15.

Royalty fee: The share of the profits made by a franchisee that is paid each year to the franchisor. (*See* **franchisee** and **franchisor**)

Salaries: Payments to employees which do not vary according to the number of hours worked or their output. A salary is usually an annual amount which is divided into 12 equal monthly instalments that the employee receives for their work each month. Salaries are an example of a fixed cost.

Stefan's annual salary was £24 000, so at the end of every month he received a monthly salary of £2000.

Sample: The people chosen to take part in primary research.

Secondary market research: Data from sources that has been collected before.

The entrepreneur used government statistics when carrying out secondary research to find out the number of people living in a particular area.

Segment: A section of a market that contains specific groups of people.

Car manufacturers divide their market to target different models at different market segments, e.g. compact cars for those living in cities.

Shareholder: An individual who owns shares in a company. They become an owner by buying a share in the business.

Sole trader: A business that is owned and controlled by one person.

A sole trader, such as a hairdresser or plumber, runs a business as an individual and is self-employed.

Solicitor: A professional who advises on legal matters relating to running a small business or a personal matter such as buying a house or managing divorce proceedings.

Sponsorship: Where a business offers financial support to an event, sports team or charity organisation in return for free advertising (e.g. sponsoring a sports team in return for the business's logo being printed on the team's shirts).

Target market: The customers that a business aims its products at.

The target market for toys is likely to be children.

Total costs: All of the costs that the business incurs for a particular level of output.

Unique selling point (USP): A feature of a business's product, service or brand (e.g. a logo) that is the only one of its kind and distinctive. It makes the product or service stand out from those of competitors.

M&Ms' unique selling point that makes it stand out from its competitors is that "the milk chocolate melts in your mouth, not in your hand".

Unlimited liability: The owner of the business is liable for the total debts of the business. If the business fails or gets into debt, the owner may be forced to sell their personal possessions to repay the business's debts.

Utilities: Services such as gas, electricity, water, internet and telephone. A business requires these services to be able to operate.

Variable costs: Costs that vary in direct proportion with changes in the level of output.

The business's variable costs included the raw materials to make the product, and packaging.

Vlog: Similar to a blog but using video. A vlogger (the author) produces visual information/video footage about a product or topic that will be of interest to followers. The footage is posted online.

Wages: A payment to employees which varies according to the number of hours worked or their output. A wage is an example of a variable cost.

The employees making the trainers are paid an hourly wage based on the number of hours they work. If they work fewer hours they are paid less, but if they work more hours they are paid more.

Well-being: The state of being healthy, happy and comfortable. Well-being can be physical or mental.

Work–life balance: The balance between the amount of time spent working and the amount of time spent on non-work activities.

Command words

Analyse: Separate or break down information into parts and identify their characteristics or elements. Explain the pros and cons of a topic or argument and make reasoned comments. Explain the impacts of actions using a logical chain of reasoning.

Annotate: Add information, for example, to a table, diagram or graph until it is final. Add all the needed or appropriate parts.

Calculate: Get a numerical answer showing how it has been worked out.

Choose: Select an answer from options given.

Circle: Select an answer from options given.

Compare and contrast: Give an account of the similarities and differences between two or more items or situations.

Complete: Add all the needed or appropriate parts. Add information, for example, to a table, diagram or graph until it is final.

Create: Produce a visual solution to a problem (for example: a mind map, flowchart or visualisation).

Describe: Give an account including all the relevant characteristics, qualities or events. Give a detailed account of.

Discuss: Present, analyse and evaluate relevant points (for example, for/against an argument).

Draw: Produce a picture or diagram.

Evaluate: Make a reasoned qualitative judgement considering different factors and using available knowledge/experience.

Explain: Give reasons for and/or causes of. Use words or phrases such as 'because', 'therefore' or 'this means' in answers.

Fill in: Add all the needed or appropriate parts. Add information, for example, to a table, diagram or graph until it is final.

Identify: Select an answer from options given. Recognise, name or provide factors or features.

Justify: Give good reasons for offering an opinion or reaching a conclusion.

Label: Add information, for example, to a table, diagram or graph until it is final. Add all the necessary or appropriate parts.

Outline: Give a short account, summary or description.

State: Give factors or features. Give short, factual answers.

Answers

The answer pages contain examples of answers that could be given to the questions from the Revision Guide and Workbook. There may be other acceptable answers.

Practise it! activities · pp. 19–65

Page 19

Any *two* from:

- Creativity – this can help the entrepreneur come up with new product ideas that are different to others on the market.

- Innovation – innovation will help the entrepreneur to think of ways to overcome issues that they encounter and to think of innovative, low-cost ways of completing tasks on a limited budget.

- Risk-taking – there is no certainty that a new venture will succeed, so an entrepreneur must be willing to take risks when setting up a new business. The entrepreneur faces the risk that the money invested will be lost.

- Communication – a successful entrepreneur needs to be able to share their business idea clearly and with enthusiasm to engage others, such as investors.

- Negotiation – to move forward with their business idea, entrepreneurs often have to negotiate with lenders, manufacturers and shops, e.g. to arrange a date that they can deliver a product to a customer or agree a price with suppliers.

- Confidence – a successful entrepreneur must believe in the potential success of their business idea. They need to have the confidence to take risks and approach others so that they can turn their business idea into a reality.

- Determination – often things will not go to plan when setting up a new business, but successful entrepreneurs overcome obstacles and continue. They will persevere until they make progress and their dream of running a business becomes a reality. **(4)**

Page 20

1. Any *three* from:
   - financial
   - independence
   - self-satisfaction
   - making a difference/change. **(3)**

2. Any *one* from:
   - Financial – the entrepreneur may benefit financially from the profit generated by the business. In some cases the profit may be greater than their wage/salary from a past job and it may enable them to enjoy a more luxurious lifestyle.

   - Independence – the entrepreneur is able to make their own decisions about the business, e.g. they can choose their own working hours and holidays. They do not have to report to anyone.

   - Self-satisfaction – the entrepreneur may find it personally rewarding to set up a successful business and to please loyal customers.

   - Making a difference/change – depending on the type of business, the entrepreneur may improve someone's life or help them. The good/service could also offer a social or environmental benefit. **(2)**

Page 21

1. Any *two* from:
   - financial
   - health/well-being
   - personal relationships. **(2)**

2 Any *one* from:
- A poor work–life balance will mean that work takes up all of the entrepreneur's time leaving them little time for physical exercise so they may become unfit and could put on weight.
- A poor work–life balance may lead to the entrepreneur having little time for hobbies which could leave them feeling stressed. **(2)**

Page 22

1 Any *one* from:
- To reduce risk – if decisions are based on the results from market research, they are more likely to lead to a successful outcome.
- To aid decision making – the information from market research can be used to make informed decisions.
- To understand the market – the results from market research will help the entrepreneur to understand their competitors, trends in the market, and customers' needs and wants.
- To gain customers' views and understand their needs/wants – by carrying out market research the entrepreneur can understand what customers want to purchase and they can develop products to meet those requirements.
- To inform product development – market research helps the entrepreneur understand what the target market thinks of the product and what might need changing to make it more desirable.
- To understand how a good/service complements others on the market – market research can help the entrepreneur to understand the products offered by competitors so that they can consider how the product that they offer compares. **(2)**

2 Market research can help an entrepreneur to develop the product/service that they offer. It will help them to understand customers' views and their needs/wants so that they can develop/

change their product ranges accordingly, which will lead to more satisfied customers. The entrepreneur will also understand the products offered by competitors so that they can consider how the products they offer compare with the competitors' products. They can then develop their own product range with differences or features that create a unique selling point (USP). **(2)**

Page 24

1 Any *two* from:
- Observations
- Questionnaires/surveys/interviews
- Focus groups
- Consumer trials
- Test marketing/pilots. **(2)**

2 **Advantages** Any *one* from:
- They can obtain in-depth information. The facilitator can question and probe the participants to gain a deeper understanding of the answers that they offer. This can lead to better decision making so that the decisions made by the entrepreneur/business are likely to be more successful/profitable.
- Participants can debate and discuss points/issues. From these discussions, the facilitator can understand whether the belief is shared by others in the group and uncover any differences in opinion. They can then discuss reasons for the differences.
- The facilitator can explain questions and/or the instructions to participants in more detail if required. This ensures that all participants fully understand the task and are likely to give more accurate information, which will enable the entrepreneur/business to make more accurate and more successful business decisions.

Disadvantages Any *one* from:
- They can be expensive and time-consuming to organise, especially if they are face to face. The organiser

needs to contact all participants and arrange a date/time that is convenient for everyone. Face-to-face focus groups may be particularly challenging to arrange as the organiser needs to book a venue in advance and participants may need to make travel arrangements. Booking a venue and paying any travel costs can increase the business's costs, which could reduce profitability.

- The group may only involve a relatively small number of participants so the data is not representative of all customers. This could result in making incorrect decisions based on a small number of potential customers and changing a product, or making other business decisions that do not suit all customers.

- Some participants may dominate discussions so not everyone contributes. This could lead to biased information as the results will only reflect the views of the dominant participants. The entrepreneur may change a product or make business decisions based on a limited number of opinions which do not reflect all customers. **(6)**

Page 25

1 Any *three* from:
- Internal data
- Books/newspapers
- Trade magazines
- Competitors' data
- Government publications and statistics
- Market research reports, e.g. Mintel or similar. **(3)**

2 Any *one* from:
- There is a vast amount of data available so it may take a long time to find the exact information required. This time could be used more productively on other tasks within the business.

- Some data could be biased to support the government's viewpoint. This may lead to inaccurate decisions, e.g. those that do not suit all customers.

- Data may be out of date, e.g. the UK Census is only done once every ten years. This may lead to decisions that do not accurately reflect current market trends/ customer preferences. **(2)**

Page 26

(c) Information is up to date. **(1)**

Page 27

1 Any *one* from:
- It can help entrepreneurs to gain a more detailed insight into the views of customers. Customers are encouraged to explain their answers, which enables the entrepreneur to understand the reasons for their answer. This can help them make more successful product/ business decisions.

- It can provide valuable information when developing a product. Qualitative data can give the entrepreneur detailed opinions, which can help them understand how to develop/change a product to better appeal to customers. **(2)**

2 • Easy to analyse
- Can be presented as graphs/charts. **(2)**

Page 28

1 Any *two* from:
- Age – the watch could be smaller, to fit the smaller wrist of a child. It could include a cartoon character and/or bright colours to appeal to a child. Or it could be more formal to appeal to an adult, e.g. a plain leather/gold/silver strap with a non-graphical face.

- Gender – the watch could have a smaller face to appeal more to females; whereas a watch for a male could have a larger face. The colours of the watch could target specific genders.

- Income – a basic watch could be sold at a low price for those on a lower income. Or the watch could include lots of features (such as a smart watch with email access, a calendar, etc.), be made of solid gold/silver and have a higher price to target those with a higher income.

- Location – the watch packaging and instructions may be written in the language of the country in which it will be sold.

- Lifestyle – a smart, hi-tech watch may appeal to someone with a business lifestyle, someone interested in a healthy lifestyle or an innovator interested in owning the latest technology. For example, it may have specific features, such as:
  - an online calendar with alerts and access to emails for a business person
  - the ability to measure the user's pulse rate or a pedometer to count the number of steps that they take.

- Occupation – specialist versions of the watch could be created to meet specific occupational requirements. For example, an athlete would require a watch with specialist functions to measure important stats, a swimmer or diver would need a waterproof watch; a business manager or someone who does a lot of international travel for work would prefer a watch that can show different time zones; and finally someone who works in a physically demanding job role, such as a construction worker, would require a highly durable design so that the watch can withstand dusty/hazardous conditions. **(4)**

2   Lifestyle. **(1)**

Page 30

1   Rent is a fixed cost because the amount that a business has to pay does not vary/change with the number of units produced/sold. The business has to pay the same rent for its factory whether it makes 500 units or 800 units per month.

Individual answers will vary depending on the fixed cost chosen. Other examples of fixed costs are: advertising, insurance, loan interest, salaries, utilities (e.g. gas, electricity, water). **(2)**

2   Total fixed costs per year:
£650 × 12 months = £7800 **(2)**

Page 31

- Total variable cost = £150 + £500 + £200
  = £850
- Variable cost per unit = £850 ÷ 50
  = £17 per unit **(2)**

Page 32

- Fixed costs per month = £48 000 ÷ 12
  = £4000
- Total cost per month = £4000 + £3000
  = £7000 **(2)**

Page 33

1   Number of units sold = £76.50 ÷ £0.75
  = 102 cupcakes **(2)**

2   Total revenue per year = £360 × 52 weeks
  = £18 720 **(2)**

Page 35

1
- Total costs = £1840 + £1200 = £3040
- Profit/loss = £3689 − £3040 = £649 **(2)**

2   Profit/loss per year = £649 × 12 months
  = £7788 **(1)**

Page 36

1   Josh will make a profit in June. He has sold 350 more cards than the break-even quantity.
Break-even quantity = £4000 ÷ (£2.50 − £0.90)
  = 2500 cards **(3)**

2   Profit = £560 **(1)**

Page 37

1
- Line 1 = Total revenue
- Line 2 = Total cost
- Line 3 = Fixed costs **(3)**

2   Any two from:
- It will tell them how many units they need to sell to make a profit. Based on the sales forecast, the entrepreneur can decide whether the business is likely to make a profit or a loss.

- It can support an application for a bank loan or help with getting investment from an investor.
- It can help to identify any costs that the business needs to reduce. The break-even graph can be changed to show the impact of reducing a specific cost.
- It can help with deciding what price to charge for a product. The break-even graph can be changed to show the impact of increasing/reducing the price. **(2)**

Page 39

1 **(a)** Money in the business's bank account/till. **(1)**

2 Any *one* from:
- To pay its bills (e.g. utilities) and employees' wages/salaries. If the business does not pay these, the utilities will be cut off/employees will stop working.
- To repay debts and loans. Lenders/creditors will chase the business for money and take legal action to reclaim the money they are owed.
- To buy materials to make products. Suppliers will stop supplying the business if it does not pay them for materials. **(2)**

3 Any *one* from:
- Without sufficient cash, the business will be forced to stop trading. Suppliers will stop supplying the business; lenders and creditors may take the business to court to force it to pay the money owed.
- Negative reputation. Word will spread that the business is unable to pay its expenses and customers may not want to purchase from the business. **(2)**

Page 40

1 Price, product, place, promotion. **(4)**

2 All elements of the marketing mix should be aligned. A high price for the can of beans does not complement other parts of the marketing mix, e.g. the economy beans are made from low-cost ingredients and the product is sold in a discount shop. The customer would not feel happy paying a high price for an economy product. They would see it as 'poor value for money', especially if they compared the product with others on the market. **(2)**

Page 42

1 Any *one* from:
- By advertising in magazines related to specific interests, gender, lifestyle, hobbies, etc., a business can target specific market segments.
- Colourful adverts increase impact, and photos can showcase the product. This can increase the appeal of the product to potential customers and therefore increase sales.
- Magazines are often widely shared (e.g. in doctor's waiting rooms, hairdressers, between friends and family) which increases the number of people who see the advert.
- Magazines can have a long lifespan, e.g. many titles publish issues on a monthly basis so magazines can be read a number of weeks after they have been published.
- Advertising in a magazine can help the product develop a specific image in line with the magazine title, e.g. if a product is advertised in a fashion magazine, the brand will be associated with high fashion. **(2)**

2 Any *one* from:
- Listeners may not take in all of the key information.
- The advert may be less than a minute long, limiting the amount of detailed information that can be included.
- Many listeners are 'passive' listeners and either change stations during the adverts or have the radio on in the background, e.g. in the car.
- Production costs may be high.
- Adverts at peak listening times are more expensive. **(2)**

Page 43

1 Any *one* from:
- Cinema adverts can be expensive to produce and are likely to be too expensive for smaller businesses.
- Many cinema goers arrive after the adverts or talk through them, so they miss them or do not engage with them, and the advertising is wasted on them and is unlikely to increase awareness.
- Whilst cinema advertising is effective for targeting some types of customers, it is not as effective for targeting customers who are less likely to visit the cinema. If the soft-drink advert is played before the wrong type of film, the advert will not be seen by the target group of customers. **(2)**

2 Any *one* from:
- Can include a photo/image of the burger to attract customers.
- Can be placed in a range of locations close to the restaurant location and/or that is access by the target customers.
- Can create an eye catching design. **(2)**

Page 46

1 Any *one* from:
- It can be too time-consuming for a small business to create a vlog as well as other advertising.
- Some customers may not have time to engage with lengthier vlogs.
- A professional vlog can be expensive to produce. **(1)**

2 Any *two* from:
- They can be cheaper than advertising through non-digital advertising mediums because there are no printing costs and no costs for distributing the advert etc. Digital adverts can often be updated quickly and cheaply, which leaves money available for other uses, e.g. additional advertising.
- Adverts can include video, audio and links to other websites/pages etc. which can increase the amount of information and the impact of the advert. This should lead to greater awareness and/or appeal to customers resulting in higher sales.
- They can target specific customers. Many digital mediums appeal to specific target markets and are therefore an effective way of targeting particular customers. The advertising budget can therefore be used more efficiently as it will not be wasted targeting customers outside the target market. **(6)**

Page 49

1 Any *one* from:
- To attract new customers to buy a product
- To retain existing customers/ encourage loyalty
- To enhance the brand's profile/reputation
- To help launch a new product
- To offer a short-term boost to sales. **(2)**

2 Any *two* from:
- Point-of-sale advertising is generally not suitable for high-cost items as people do not 'impulse' buy them.
- As point of sale is commonly used to advertise low-price products, it generates low revenue.
- Most retailers only have limited space for point-of-sale advertising so only a limited range of products can benefit from being promoted in this way. **(4)**

Page 50

1 Any *two* from:
- Product placement
- Celebrity endorsement
- Press/media releases. **(2)**

2 Any *two* from:
- The press release may generate free publicity for the school. Often schools have limited promotion budgets. Free publicity

means that the school can use the budget for other purposes, e.g. additional advertising alongside the press release to give the school greater public exposure.

- The local newspaper may visit and take photos of the new science block so the coverage in the newspaper may be extensive and generate additional interest within the local community. This will increase public awareness of the story/school/new science block.

- The school can target the local community effectively and make the local residents aware of the story/school/new science block. As the newspaper is only available within the local area, it will be read by local residents.

- Many local newspapers also publish stories on the newspaper's website. This can generate additional coverage and target other people who may not read the printed newspaper. The school will therefore benefit from targeting a larger group of readers.

- Other local newspapers and media organisations may see the article and also want to cover the story. This could result in publicity across a number of different newspapers/advertising mediums, such as the local television news or local radio. This will result in greater coverage of the story and it will reach a wider audience than just the readers of the local newspaper.

- As the story has been written by an independent journalist rather than the school itself, readers may perceive it as being unbiased. People may be more likely to read and take an interest in the story as it is an independent journalist saying how good the school's facilities are, rather than the school itself. **(6)**

Page 51

1   Any *one* from:
- Reduced overheads/costs for the business. The business generally has to pay lower fixed costs for a digital channel, e.g. no shop rent, fewer staff required,

no electricity/gas needed to heat/light a shop. Reducing overheads and expenses will lead to increased profitability (assuming all the revenue and other expenses remain the same).

- To offer greater convenience for customers. Digital channels are available 24 hours a day so consumers can purchase whenever they want.

- Digital channels can serve customers across a wider geographic area. The business can therefore sell to customers across a wider area, which will lead to increased revenue. **(2)**

2   Any *one* from:
- It is often easier for the bank to develop a relationship with customers via the branch staff who serve customers on a face-to-face basis. They can have conversations with customers which may reveal life events that provide an opportunity for the bank to sell additional products, e.g. someone may be thinking of moving house and branch staff can make the customer aware of the range of mortgages that the bank offers.

- Some customers may be unable to bank online or may not be comfortable banking online. By retaining branches, the bank can serve the needs of a greater number of customers and retain customers who prefer to bank 'in person'.

- The physical signs (e.g. outside the bank) and posters in the windows can promote the bank's brand and its products and services. Customers passing the branch are made aware of the brand from the signs, and of new products and services (e.g. savings accounts or types of insurance) by the posters. They may go on to purchase the products/services advertised in the posters, thereby increasing the bank's revenue.

- It can be more convenient or quicker for a customer to walk into a branch and ask the member of staff rather than waiting in a queue for telephone banking or explaining the issue to a computerised online help function. Customers are likely to value this 'personalised' contact and may remain loyal to the bank. (3)

Page 53

1
- Product A – Introduction
- Product B – Decline
- Product C – Growth
- Product D – Maturity (4)

2 Profitability of Product A may be low at the end of Year 4 because it has only just been launched onto the market. As customers may not be aware of the product, revenue is very low. Revenue is not yet sufficient to recover the high costs of developing the product and promoting its launch. (3)

Page 55

The following three are exemplar answers. Individual student answers may vary depending on the extension strategies chosen.

1 Two extension strategies are advertising and reducing the price of the soft drink, e.g. a fruit-flavoured drink produced by Zero Drinks. The drink could be advertised more, maybe using different/additional mediums, to raise awareness and stimulate new sales. The drink could be given a new slogan within the adverts. The price of the drink could also be reduced. For example, it could be reduced by 20 percent, which may mean that it is cheaper than other drinks on the market, which could stimulate sales. (4)

2 Increased advertising may remind existing customers about the drink which could encourage them to buy it. It could also make new customers aware of it for the first time and encourage them to try it. However, advertising could be very expensive. A lower price may make the drink more affordable so more customers can afford to buy it, which could increase sales. The reduced price may make the drink more appealing than rival drinks so Zero Drinks may benefit from customers switching from another brand. However, reducing the price may also reduce the amount of revenue that it generates. (6)

3 I would recommend reducing the price. Although advertising could help to increase the sales of the drinks, the additional revenue from increased sales may not cover the cost of the advertising. Zero Drinks will need to attract a lot of additional sales to cover the advertising costs. By reducing the price, although Zero Drinks will generate less revenue for each drink that it sells, the reduced price may result in a significant increase in sales. Therefore, the total revenue may be higher than selling it at the original higher price. Higher total revenue may result in greater profitability (if all other costs remain unchanged). (8)

Page 56

Any one from:

- The income level of target customers will determine what they can afford to pay. If the price is unaffordable, sales of the product are likely to be very low.

- Price is often one of the first things that a customer considers when buying a product. Customers use price to compare the product with others on the market and to assess whether they think it is worth the amount that is being charged. (2)

Page 57

1 A low price encourages customers to take a risk and try the new product, e.g. a new shampoo from AB Haircare. Customers may be loyal to another more well-known brand of shampoo and may be reluctant to try something new, especially if they are unfamiliar with the AB Haircare brand name. A low price can tempt customers to try the new shampoo. They may then become loyal to AB Haircare if they find that the new shampoo is better than their usual one. These customers will then be willing to pay a higher price when the price is increased. (2)

2 • Initially, the company, e.g. AB Haircare which is launching a new shampoo, might make a loss or a low profit. The low price may not cover the costs of producing the shampoo or may result in the profit margin being low.

  • There is no guarantee that customers will continue to purchase the shampoo when the price increases. When the price increases, customers may return to their former brand.

  • A competitor may reduce its prices and could undercut the price of the shampoo. It could start a price war. **(3)**

Page 60

1 Any *three* from:
  • Partnership
  • Limited liability partnership
  • Private limited company (Ltd)
  • Franchise **(3)**

2 The sole trader can make all decisions for the business (1). This means that the owner does not have to consult anyone regarding decisions (1) so they can run the business as they wish (1).

  A sole trader is relatively easy to set up (1). There is less paperwork to complete to set up this type of business (1) which means that setting one up is less stressful/time consuming (1).

  A sole trader can keep all profit made (1). The profits do not have to be shared with other owners (1) so they may earn a greater financial reward (1). **(6)**

Page 61

Advantages Any *one* from:

  • The business has a greater chance of success as the business brand/name is already known. Customers will already recognise the brand, and because of loyalty/familiarity/reputation will be more likely to purchase from the 'new' business.

  • The franchisee is supported by the franchisor (e.g. with advice and training).

This can increase the chances of success as the franchisee is less likely to make inappropriate decisions.

  • The franchisee only requires limited industry knowledge as they are following the franchisor's business model and training.

Disadvantages Any *one* from:

  • The franchisor will make all of the key decisions regarding the business.

  • The franchisee will have to pay a share of the profit made each year to the franchisor.

  • It can be expensive to become a franchisee. **(4)**

Page 62

1 **(b)** Partnership **(1)**

2 Partnership (but not a limited liability partnership) and sole trader. **(2)**

3 Any *one* from:
  • The amount that the owner can potentially lose is limited, so they cannot lose any more money than they originally invested. This can provide peace of mind for the owner.

  • The owner cannot be forced to sell any of their personal possessions, such as their house or car, to repay business debts. This can make the owner more confident about starting in the business as there is less risk. **(2)**

Page 64

1 Any *one* from:
  • It may not raise the required amount of money.

  • It can take some time to raise the required investment.

  • The entrepreneur often needs to promote the product to raise awareness and attract investors, which can take time and possibly money.

- Investors may want a share of the profit and might interfere with how the business is run. **(1)**

2 Any *one* from:
- The business does not have to pay interest or fees. It can therefore use all of the capital that the entrepreneur has saved up for business purposes, such as funding future growth/expansion, rather than using some of it to pay interest or fees.
- The business does not need to submit an application for the capital. This can save time and effort, leaving them time to complete other tasks within the business. Unlike a bank loan or other source of capital that the entrepreneur needs to apply for, the entrepreneur's own savings are a guaranteed source of capital.
- The entrepreneur does not need to repay the funds. The business can therefore benefit from reduced expenses, which will help its cash flow. All the capital can therefore be used for business purposes, e.g. future expansion or growth. **(3)**

Page 65

1 Solicitor. **(1)**

2 Any *two* from:
- The advice is usually provided free of charge. The advice is informal and the entrepreneur does not need to sign a contract to access the advice.
- The entrepreneur may be able to contact the family member at any time and does not need to arrange a meeting/ appointment to speak with them. This is convenient.
- The advice is likely to be unbiased, e.g. the family member will not earn a fee for providing advice or recommendations.
- As the entrepreneur knows the family member well, they may be happier asking questions than if they were asking a stranger or a formal adviser, and a family member is likely to give an honest response.
- The family member may own a small business and be able to advise based on their experience of **all** aspects of running a small business. **(4)**

Workbook pp. 66–98

Page 66

1 **(c)** Recklessness **(1)**

2 Determination – An entrepreneur will need to be determined because some plans may not work out. They will need to be committed to the business idea and keep trying new things. They cannot give up at the first setback.

Any second characteristic from:

- Creativity
- Communication
- Innovation
- Negotiation
- Risk-taking
- Confidence.

Example answer:

Risk-taking – An entrepreneur will need to be prepared to take a risk. There is no guarantee that the business will be a success. There is a risk that they may lose money invested in the business and/or waste time setting up a business which may then fail. **(4)**

3 Starting a new business is hard work and the entrepreneur is likely to have to work long hours doing all the jobs that have to be done. Working long hours will affect the entrepreneur's work–life balance as spending longer at work will leave less time for hobbies and relaxation. **(2)**

4 Any two from:

- Financial
- Independence
- Self-satisfaction
- Making a difference/change.

Example answers:

Independence – The entrepreneur is free to make their own decisions and they will not have to answer to anyone else. They will be able to choose their own working hours and enjoy greater freedom.

Financial – The entrepreneur may make a greater profit from the business than the salary that they previously earned. This will enable them to enjoy a more lavish lifestyle. **(4)**

Page 67

1 **(d)** Secondary **(1)**

2 Any *two* from:

- To reduce risk.
- To aid decision making.
- To understand the market.
- To gain customers' views and understand their needs/wants.
- To inform product development.
- To understand how a good/service complements others on the market. **(2)**

3 Any *one* from:

- Data is for the entrepreneur's sole use (it cannot be seen by competitors).
- Data is normally more up to date than secondary data as it has not been published.
- The market research can be tailored to the needs of the business and the type of product offered. **(1)**

4 **(b)** Primary research **(1)**

5 Any *two* from:

- Official statistics are likely to be accurate and reliable (1 mark: point). This will result in Rani basing her decisions on accurate data and therefore her decisions are likely to be more successful (1 mark: explanation) leading to increased sales revenue (1 mark: impact).
- A lot of data is available covering a wide range of topics (1). Rani is likely to be able to gain a thorough understanding of her market (1). She is likely to be able to answer most questions that she would like to answer (1).

- The statistics are normally free to access (1). This will save Rani money (1) which is important as she is unlikely to have a large market research budget as she is still planning her business. The funds saved can be used for other purposes within the business (1).
- The statistics are easy to access (1) online. Rani only needs access to the internet so she can quickly (1) download the statistics at a time convenient (1) to her and from any location. **(6)**

6 Any *two* from:
   - Internal data, e.g. sales reports
   - Books
   - Newspapers
   - Trade magazines
   - Competitors' data
   - Market research reports, e.g. Mintel. **(2)**

Page 68

1 You get one mark for correctly identifying an advantage/disadvantage and one mark for an explanation of each advantage/disadvantage.

   Advantages Any *one* from:
   - Easy to access and generally fairly low cost. This will save the business's market research budget and leave more money that can be spent on other things such as projects or research to benefit the business.
   - Trade magazines usually focus on a specific industry. The articles are likely to be specialised and detailed and so give the entrepreneur a detailed insight into the industry.

   Disadvantages Any *one* from:
   - The information in newspapers may be too general and not relevant so it may be of limited benefit to the entrepreneur. This could waste their time which could have been spent on more productive projects or tasks.
   - The information in books may be out of date as information may change after the book has been published. This will limit the success of any decisions made as they are not based on current trends in the market.
   - May be biased or inaccurate which will limit the success of any decisions made. **(4)**

2 You get one mark for correctly identifying an advantage/disadvantage, one mark for an explanation of each advantage/disadvantage, and one mark for impact.

   Advantages Any *one* from:
   - One advantage of conducting primary market research is that it is tailored to Louis' business idea (1). Louis can design the questions so that he gets the information he needs (1). The impact of this on the business is that the information is completely relevant for Louis' business idea, so any decisions made using the information are more likely to be successful (1).
   - Primary market research will be carried out by Louis now (1) so the information collected will be up to date (1). This will increase the likely success of decisions made using this information (1).
   - The results from primary market research will only be available for Louis (1) so competitors will not be able to access the information (1). Louis may be able to create a USP/competitive advantage (1).

   Disadvantages Any *one* from:
   - It will be more time-consuming (1) for Louis to gather primary market research as he has to plan and carry out the market research. The results will also have to be analysed (1). This may leave Louis less time for other tasks involved in setting up/running the small shop (1).
   - Primary market research is often more expensive (1) than secondary market research. This is due to the time that it takes to plan, carry out and analyse the information (1). This will leave Louis less money for other purposes (1).

- As a shop owner, Louis may not have the skills (1) to plan, carry out and analyse the information, which could lead to information that is biased as Louis may focus on just one element of the answers given (1). Biased results may have a negative effect on business decisions (1). **(6)**

Page 69

1 Quantitative data is data expressed as numbers or facts (1). It can be quantified, for instance the number of people who offered a response, or the proportion of a market research sample that agreed with a statement (1).

Qualitative data is data expressed as opinions and views (1). It is relatively more challenging to analyse than quantitative data but can provide more in-depth information as it considers people's motives and reasons (1). **(4)**

2 Any *two* of the following:
- Internal numerical data
- Competitors' numerical data
- Government statistics
- Data within a market research report, such as Mintel
- Numerical data published within a book/ newspaper/trade magazine. **(2)**

3 Any *one* of the following:
- It is quick to analyse because it is numerical data.
- The data can be presented visually in the form of a graph/chart which can make it easier to understand.
- The numbers can be converted to percentages or fractions. **(2)**

4 You get one mark for correctly identifying an advantage/limitation and a further one mark for an explanation of each advantage/limitation.

Advantages Any *one* from:
- The entrepreneur will gain a more detailed insight into the views of customers which will help them make more successful/informed decisions.
- The data is very detailed.
- The data is likely to include information about the customers' conversations/ discussions that took place at the focus group.

Limitations Any *one* from:
- May be relatively expensive as the views of fewer customers are likely be included in the data.
- May be more subject to bias due to fewer customers' views being reflected in the data.
- More challenging to analyse and find patterns/trends in the data. The data is in a non-numerical format. **(4)**

Page 70

1 **(c)** Dividing a market by lifestyle, gender, age, etc. **(1)**

2 **(e)** Income **(1)**

3 **(d)** To meet different customers' needs **(1)**

4 **(a)** Any *two* from:
- Age
- Gender
- Income
- Lifestyle
- Location. **(2)**

(b) Any *two* from:

- Ensures that the needs of the target customers are matched and met. The product can better appeal to their requirements and profile. That may increase sales revenue which could support increased profitability (if costs remain unchanged).
- Money is not wasted promoting the product in ways that would not appeal to the target customers and/or

the product is designed to effectively appeal to the target customers.

- The marketing mix elements can be targeted to the target customers, e.g. advertising can be designed in a way to appeal to the target customers and the advertising mediums would appeal to the target customers which will increase sales revenue.
- Customers are less likely to choose competing products if the product offered meets their needs. This will increase customer retention with benefits to the sales revenue generated.
- Market share is likely to increase as sales will increase (benefiting sales revenue). Customers will remain loyal to a product that meets their needs and other customers from the target market may leave competitors and purchase the product instead. **(4)**

Page 71

1 Variable costs are costs that change (1) in line with changes to the number of products made/produced or sold (1). One further mark for an example. Examples include:
- Raw materials/components
- Packaging
- Wages. **(3)**

2 **(d)** Variable costs **(1)**

3 Fixed costs:
- Rent
- Loan interest (only the interest is a cost and not the capital repaid)
- Advertising
- Insurance
- Utilities, e.g. gas, electricity.

Variable costs:
- Wages for the part-time employees
- Packaging for the furniture
- Raw materials, e.g. wood
- Components. **(6)**

4 **(a)** Variable costs = total costs − variable costs

Variable costs = £4500 − £3000
= £1500 per month **(1)**

(b) Fixed costs per year = Fixed costs per month × 12 months

Fixed costs per year = £3000 × 12 months
= £36 000 **(1)**

Page 72

1 The fixed costs are:

Rent: £300

Utilities: £50

Salaries: £600

Total fixed costs = £300 + £50 + £600
= £950 per month **(1)**

2 The variable costs are:

Ingredients: £2.30 × 1350 = £3105 (1)

Packaging: £0.50 × 1350 = £675 (1)

Total variable costs = £3105 + £675 = £3780 (1)

(3)

3 Total costs = fixed costs + variable costs

Total costs per month = £950 + £3780
= £4730 (1)

Total costs per year = £4730 × 12 months
= £56 760 (1)

(2)

4 Total costs = fixed costs + variable costs

Variable costs for 950 slices of cake:
Ingredients − £2.30 × 950 = £2185 (1)

Packaging − £0.50 × 950 = £475 (1)

Total variable costs = £2185 + £475 = £2660 (1)

Total costs = £950 + £2660 (1)
(4)

Pages 73–74

1 **(d)** Selling price per unit × number of sales **(1)**

2 Total revenue is the amount of money that a business earns from selling its products (1).

Total revenue expresses the revenue generated from selling a specific number of products. It is calculated by the formula: selling price per unit × number of items sold (1). **(2)**

3 **(a)** Total revenue = selling price per unit × number sales

Revenue for luxury party bags
= £5.99 × 30 bags = £179.70 (1)

Revenue for standard party bags
= £3.50 × 50 bags = £175.00 (1)

Total revenue = £179.70 + £175.00
              = £354.50 (1)

(3)

(b) Total revenue for the year
= average revenue per week
  × 52 weeks (1)

Total revenue for the year
= £354.50 × 52 weeks = £18 434 (1)

(2)

(c) Total revenue = selling price per unit × number sales

Revenue for standard party bags
= £4.99 × 48 bags = £239.52 (1)

Revenue for the 4-week period
= £239.52 × 4 weeks = £958.08 (1)

(2)

4 **(a)** **(ii)** 240 **(1)**

(b) Average selling price
= total revenue ÷ number of sales (1)

Average selling price
= £1350 ÷ 25 = £54 (1)

(2)

Page 75

1 **(d)** £15 000 **(1)**

2 **(b)** Loss **(1)**

3 **(a)** Total cost per week = £150 + £450 + £25
                          + £200 = £825 (1)

Total costs per month = £825 × 4 weeks
                      = £3300 (1)

(2)

(b) Profit = revenue − total costs (1)

Profit = £13 500 − £3300 = £10 200 (1)

(2)

(c) Profit = revenue − total costs (1)

Revenue = profit + total costs (1)

Revenue = £20 500 + £3300 = £23 800 (1)

(3)

Pages 76–77

1 Break-even = fixed costs ÷ (selling price per
                          unit − variable cost per unit)

Break-even = £225 ÷ (£40 − £23) (1)
           = £225 ÷ £17
           = 14 units (1)

Only 1 mark can be offered if the answer is not rounded up, e.g. 13.24 units. **(2)**

2 Break-even = £310 ÷ (£40 − £23) (1)
            = 19 units (1)

Claire will have to sell an additional 5 units (1)

A maximum of 2 marks for answers that do not include rounded-up figures. **(3)**

3 Selling price per unit − variable costs per unit
= fixed costs ÷ break-even quantity

? = £1260 ÷ 20

? = £63 (1)

Selling price per unit − £30 = £63 (1)

Selling price per unit = £63 + £30 (1)
                       = £93 (1)

(4)

4 Any *one* from:

- Claire's business will make a loss.
- Claire's business will not survive in the long term as she will not be making any money. **(1)**

5 Any *three* from:

- Pay employees
- Pay for supplies of raw materials
- Pay rent or mortgage
- Pay utilities such as gas or electricity
- Make a loan repayment. **(3)**

Pages 78–79

1 **(b)** Total costs **(1)**

2 **(a)** Fixed costs **(1)**

3 £450 000 (answers between £440 000 and £460 000 are acceptable) **(1)**

4 Loss **(1)**

5 Profit **(1)**

6 **(d)** What price to charge **(1)**

Page 79

1 Any *two* from:
- To pay rent / utilities
- To pay employees
- To pay for anything unexpected that could arise
- To repay debts, e.g. loan repayments
- To buy raw materials. **(2)**

2 Any *three* from:
- Customers may be offered credit terms and so pay the business a month or two after taking delivery of their order (1) which leaves the business short of cash while waiting for payment (1).
- A customer may go bankrupt (1) and fail to pay their invoices/bills for goods/ services that the business supplied and paid its suppliers for (1).
- A business may receive a large order from a customer and have to pay suppliers immediately for the raw materials required to produce the goods for the order (1). While the goods are being made the business may be short of cash as no cash will be received from the customer until the order is delivered (1).
- The business may have paid for a large amount of stock (1) which it now cannot sell because it has gone out of date or is obsolete so needs to be disposed of (1).
- The business's supplier may insist on payment upon delivery of supplies (1), but customers may be offered credit terms so they do not pay the business immediately for products supplied (1). **(6)**

Page 80

1 **(a)** Packaging **(1)**

2 Price **(1)**

3 Any *one* of the following for price:
- The low price may make customers think that Karlton's products are poorer quality (1) than those offered by competitors if the price is much lower (1). This will give Karlton's products a negative image/ reputation (1).
- The low price is limiting the profit that Karlton makes on each product sold. His profit margin will be low (1) and this is contributing to the low profitability of his product (1). The price must cover the cost of production and leave enough for a profit (1).
- Customers may think that the low price is too good to be true (1) and could be wary that it is a con, thus reducing sales (1). Customers often compare the prices of similar products to decide if a price is reasonable (1).

Any *one* of the following for product:
- The product is aimed at professional sports players (1) and should be priced to appeal to the prestigious market (1). Price indicates the potential quality (1).
- The product is a core element of the marketing mix as it is the item that the customer is buying (1). The other elements of the marketing mix help to create a specific brand image (1) such as premium or economy (1). **(6)**

Pages 81–82

1 **Type of advertising medium** — **Description**

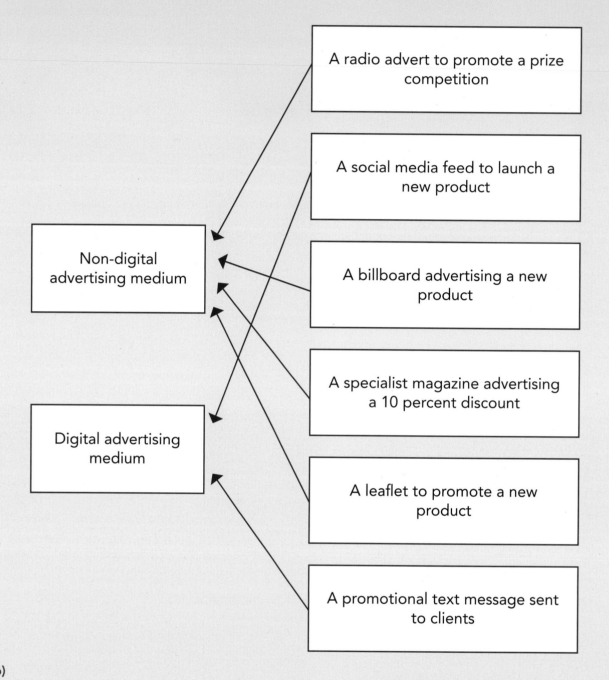

(6)

2 Any *two* from:

- Social media
- Websites
- Online banners/pop-ups
- SMS texts
- Podcasts
- Vlogs/blogs
- Email. **(2)**

3 Any *two* from:

- Radio stations are often targeted at specific segments of the market (1). This will help the business to target the type of customers that the product is aimed at (1). This reduces wastage as a high proportion of listeners would be interested in the product (1), therefore increasing sales.

- Can use audio/music/jingles (1) to increase awareness and catch listeners' attention. A catchy jingle or well-known song is likely to 'stick' in a listener's head therefore increasing recall of the advert and the product (1), increasing sales (1).
- Radio adverts may be repeated (1) a number of times during the day. Repeated exposure to the advert will increase the listeners' awareness (1) of an advert/product, increasing sales (1). **(6)**

Pages 83–84

1 **(a)** Any *two* from:
- One drawback of using a billboard as a method of advertising is that the best (most prominent) locations to advertise in are very expensive. This might be a problem for a small business with a limited budget as they may only be able to afford to advertise in the less-prominent locations which will not be seen by as many people. The impact on the business would be that it reduces the effectiveness of the advert to attract customers.
- A billboard cannot usually include audio material. This will limit the impact of the advert. The advert may become 'background' and passers-by may ignore it. This will reduce the effectiveness of the advert to attract customers.
- Billboards are often positioned on busy roads. Although a lot of traffic will pass it, most drivers will miss the advert as they are concentrating on the road/traffic and therefore ignore it. This will reduce the effectiveness of the advert to attract customers.
- Only simple messages can be included. People will not have the time (or the resources) to read/note complex information, e.g. ingredients or telephone numbers. **(6)**

(b) Any *two* from:
- Leaflets
- Newspapers
- Magazines
- Radio
- Cinema.

'Posters' is not acceptable as they are too similar to billboards. **(2)**

2 Leaflets

Advantages	Disadvantages
• Effectively target customers in a local area, which is important for a plumber as they will only serve a relatively local area • Visually appealing and easy to read • Can include photos, graphics and lots of information • Relatively cheap to produce • Can be produced in colour or in black and white to reduce costs	• The customer may throw the leaflet away without reading it, especially if they think it is junk mail • Environmental cost of using paper • Impact is short term as leaflets are rarely kept for long

Social media

Advantages	Disadvantages

• Free/cheap way of advertising	• Not everyone is on social media, people may only use some platforms, so the business will have to advertise on multiple platforms to reach large numbers
	• Can have a short timeframe
	• May appear biased as they are written by the business
	• Unhappy followers may post negative comments, which:
	  • are hard to delete and are visible to potential customers
	  • may include exaggerated comments
	  • can have a negative impact on the business's reputation

Justification:

- The answer must identify whether either leaflets or social media are best for the plumbing business.
- Refer to the context – remember the plumber will only be able to serve a limited geographic area and is unlikely to undertake plumbing jobs in different countries or long distances from their base.

Example answer showing the marks awarded:

One advantage of using leaflets is that photos/graphics (1) can be included, which can help to attract the attention of the reader. This may have a positive impact on sales. However, the customer may throw the leaflet away before reading it as they may view it as junk mail, which will result in the advertising being a waste of money (1).

Social media is a free method of advertising (1) and the money saved can be used for other purposes in the business. However, not everyone uses social media so they may not see the advert. This will reduce the effectiveness of this form of advertising (1).

I think leaflets are best for the plumbing business (1). This is because a plumber will only operate in the local area and leaflets are good for targeting households in a specific local area (1). Social media targets users around the world (1). People in other countries or areas of the UK will not be able to benefit from the plumber's services as plumbers are unlikely to travel outside their local area due to the nature of their work (1). **(8)**

Page 85

1 **(d)** Sponsorship **(1)**

2 **(b)** Loyalty schemes **(1)**

3 Benefit:
- An exciting prize may generate a lot of additional publicity, e.g. word of mouth or social media sharing from excited customers. The publicity may gain a lot of additional sales and brand awareness which would otherwise cost a lot of money in advertising.

Any *one* limitation from:

- The prize may be expensive (1) which could then reduce the funds available for other types of promotion (1). The prize will normally have to cost a lot in order to generate interest (1).
- Additional promotion (1) will be required to make customers aware of the prize competition (1). If people are unaware of the competition it will not have the desired impact on sales (1).
- The prize may not be considered desirable by all customers (1) and therefore not generate any additional sales (1). The prize must be chosen carefully (1).
- Specific terms and conditions will need to be created (1) to support the competition and ensure fairness (1). Legal help may be required to write these terms and conditions, and that could be expensive (1). **(6)**

4 **(d)** Celebrity endorsement **(1)**

Pages 86–87

1 Physical **(1)**

2 Any *two* from:
- E-commerce
- Websites
- Social media
- Marketplace sites
- Online auction sites
- Downloads. **(2)**

3 Any *one* advantage from:
- The customer can purchase at their own convenience. Social media is available 24/7 (1) so the customer can purchase at the time most convenient (1) for them. They are not limited to specific opening hours.
- Social media posts can be updated instantly and regularly (1). Errors with the

post can be amended easily, new offers can be added, and changes can be made ensuring customers receive the latest information (1).

Any *one* disadvantage from:

- It is not as easy for the customer to speak directly to the business (1), e.g. if they have any queries about the product or need to make a complaint. This can frustrate customers (1).
- Not all customers have access to the internet (1) so the business may miss out on sales from some customers (1). This may limit their market.
- Customers cannot touch or see the actual product or try it on before buying it (1). This may result in the business having to accept more returns which can be costly to administer (1).
- Customers have to wait a few days to receive their goods (1) which may put off some customers if they would like the product immediately. This may limit sales (1). **(4)**

4 Any *two* from:

- The product range is expensive. There are likely to be cheaper alternatives available from other retailers and the retailer wants to physically demonstrate its products (1) to customers to help them understand why they should buy from them (and possibly spend more money) (1).
- The retailer is able to build a relationship with customers more easily on a face-to-face basis (1). This will help the customer to trust the retailer and increase the likelihood of them buying (1).
- The customer can see the actual product before buying (1), e.g. sit on a sofa before purchase so they can be confident that it is comfortable (1).
- The sales staff can offer additional information about the product, e.g. observations based on their experience and/or answer customer questions immediately (1) which can tempt them to purchase (1). **(4)**

5 **Physical channels**

Advantages	Disadvantages
• Face-to-face contact builds customer trust • Customers can see or try the product they are buying (e.g. trying on a jacket to check the fit) • Sales staff can demonstrate the features and benefits of a product (e.g. a high-specification television with surround sound)	• More expensive than selling online as businesses have to pay rent on high street shops • Customers have to travel to a shop, which takes time, and they may have problems with parking if they drive there • Opening hours can be more limited as most shops are unable to open 24 hours a day due to trading laws

Digital channels

Advantages	Disadvantages
• Reduced costs, such as rent, as businesses do not need physical shops • Prices may be lower as the business does not have to pay rent on a physical shop • Customers can shop at any time of the day or night	• It is not as easy for the customer to speak directly to the business, e.g. if they have any queries about the product or need to make a complaint • Not all customers have access to the internet • Customers cannot touch or see the actual product or try it on before buying it • Customers have to wait a few days to receive their goods

Justification:

- The answer must identify if either physical or digital channels are best for Narinder's business.
- Refer to the context – remember Narinder's business sells samosas.

Example answer showing the marks awarded:

If Narinder sells via physical channels he will be able to build up a relationship with his customers (1) which will help customers to trust his business and become more loyal. However, Narinder's operating costs may be higher as he will have to pay rent/rates on his premises which may then reduce his profits, or he may decide to increase the prices that he charges customers to cover the increased expenses (1).

Narinder could sell via digital channels which can increase customer convenience as they can purchase 24/7 (1). However, not all customers have access to the internet so he may find that some customers cannot purchase from his business if he operates solely digitally (1).

I think Narinder should choose physical channels (1). His business will service customers in the local area and he can demonstrate the features of his samosas and why they are better than competitors' (1). Digital channels do not often allow customers to contact the business easily (1) and Narinder will be unable to obtain feedback from customers to develop new recipes to further the success of his business (1). **(8)**

Pages 88–89

1 **(b)** Boom **(1)**

2 **(a)** The diagram should be labelled as follows:

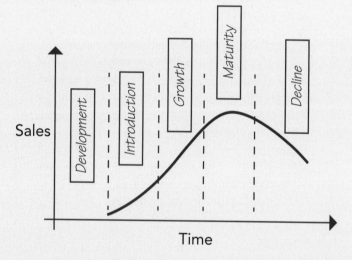

(5)

(b) Growth **(1)**

(c) Any *one* from:

- Pricing changes. The price of the product may change to stimulate more sales as the product moves through the product lifecycle, e.g. the price may reduce as the product moves into decline to make it more affordable and therefore generate more sales.

- Promotion decisions. The product may be promoted more or in different ways to stimulate more sales as it progresses through the product lifecycle.

- Place decisions. The product may start to be offered in new/additional places to stimulate more sales as it moves through the product lifecycle, e.g. the product may be offered in additional places to help sales grow whilst in the growth stage.

- Product decisions. The recipe of the product may change to generate more sales. **(2)**

(d) Any *two* from:

- Advertising. The product may be promoted more or in different ways to stimulate more sales.

- Price changes. The price of the product may increase/decrease to generate more sales. The price often changes as the product moves through the product lifecycle.

- Adding value. The recipe of the product may change to generate more sales, or new flavours may be introduced to appeal to new types of customers, e.g. a vegan product range could be launched to appeal to vegan customers.

- Exploring new markets. The product may be offered in new geographic areas, or to new target markets, to stimulate additional sales.

- New packaging. New packaging may make customers think that the product has changed and therefore purchase it. The new packaging may appeal to new customer groups. **(4)**

Pages 90–91

1 **(b)** Price skimming **(1)**

2 **(a)** Setting a low price at the start to encourage people to purchase, then increasing the price after the introductory period. **(1)**

(b) Any *one* advantage from the following.

- The low price will:
    - encourage customers to try the new product (1) and build interest in the product which will help increase sales (1)
    - encourage customers to try the new product (1) and help it become established and increase market share (1)
    - create customer loyalty (1) as they cannot find a cheaper alternative (1)
    - increase sales (1) as customers switch from competing brands, as long as the product is better (1).
- The low price is only for a short period (1), so revenue and profits should recover over time (1).

Any *one* disadvantage from the following:
- A low price:
    - means lower revenue (1) and profits in the short term (1)
    - may not persuade customers to switch from another product that they trust and are loyal to (1) as it is not worth the risk for a small financial gain (1)
    - may create an image of a poor-quality product (1) as often customers associate the quality with the price paid (1)
    - may not cover the costs of production (1) and may result in the business making a loss (1).
- Some customers may only buy when the price is low (1), and return to competitor products when the price increases to normal (1).
- Customers may be unhappy when the price increases (1) and purchase from other businesses instead (1). **(4)**

3 Psychological pricing. **(1)**

4 The business sets a price in line with that of competitors (1) so the cards are no cheaper but are no more expensive than those of competitors (1). **(2)**

5 Any *two* of the following:
- Income of the target audience (1). An entrepreneur needs to know how much the target audience earns so that they can set the price of the product at an amount that the target audience can afford so they will be able to purchase it, therefore increasing sales (1).
- Price of competitor products (1). If the product is much more expensive than identical products sold by rivals, customers will choose their product as they will feel that the product is a rip-off or a con (1).

    OR
- Price of competitor products (1). If the product is much cheaper than those offered by competitors customers may fear that the quality is much lower and/or that it is a con which may put them off buying it (1).
- Cost of production (1). The price charged must fully cover the cost of production otherwise the entrepreneur will make a loss for every product sold, which will eventually put them out of business (1).
- Stage of the product lifecycle (1). The price of the product will often change as the product moves through the lifecycle to generate additional sales and/or maximise profits (1). **(4)**

Page 92

1 Competitive pricing

Advantages	Disadvantages
• As the price is in line with that of competitors, customers will be willing to pay it • Prevents competitors from having a price advantage	• Can lead to low prices and low profits • Low prices may not cover the costs of production and may result in the business making a loss • May be difficult for a small business to set prices at the same level as large competitors who can often buy supplies cheaper as they buy larger quantities • Regular market research is required to keep up to date with the prices charged by competitors • If the business sells online to customers around the world, it will be hard to price match every business • Could lead to a price war if the competitor is keen to maintain a price advantage in the market (i.e. offer the lowest-price product within the market)

Psychological pricing

Advantages	Disadvantages
• The selling price is only reduced slightly, which will not have a significant effect on revenue • As customers may have a limited budget, they may view the product as being better value/more affordable • Attracts customer attention as £1.99 has more of an impact than £2	• As this is a common pricing strategy, the product will not stand out if all of the competitors are also doing it • Customers may feel like they are being taken advantage of • Customers might see the product as being low quality • There is no guarantee that it will increase sales (i.e. if more customers do not purchase the product, revenue will be reduced)

Justification:

- The answer must identify if either competitive pricing or psychological pricing is most appropriate for the ready-meal business.
- Refer to the context – remember that ready-meals are a competitive market as customers have lots of options, e.g. getting a ready-meal from the supermarket, ordering a takeaway or visiting a restaurant.

Example answer showing the marks awarded:

Competitive pricing ensures that no competitor has a price advantage over the product as rival products will be the same price, which ensures that sales are not lost based on price alone (1). However, competing businesses might be large and benefit from lower operating costs due to the volume of items produced/sold. They may be able to charge low prices, and if a new business charges the same price the operating costs may not be covered resulting in a loss (1).

Psychological pricing is an easy way of making the product appear cheaper which may help to attract customers and boost sales (1). However, competitors may use the same pricing strategy so the product may not stand out as being cheaper (1).

I believe competitive pricing is the best option (1) as there are a lot of businesses offering vegan meals. Competitive pricing ensures that competitors do not have a price advantage (1). Psychological pricing will not have a large impact as customers are not going to switch from a meal they enjoy to save a few pence (1) so it will not have any impact on sales (1). **(8)**

Pages 93–94

1   **(a)** A sole trader is a business that is owned by one person, i.e. the sole trader. They make all the decisions themselves and have unlimited liability. **(2)**

   (b) Any *two* from:

   - Partnership
   - Limited liability partnership
   - Private limited company
   - Franchise (become a franchisee). **(2)**

(c) Any *one* from:

- Can keep all profits made (1). Do not have to share profits with any other owners (1).
- The sole trader is their own boss and can make all the business decisions (1). They have the freedom to make decisions as they wish. There is no one to disagree with them. Decisions can therefore be made quicker (1).
- Relatively cheap and easy to set up (i.e. no complex paperwork) (1) which can make setting up the business more accessible (1).
- May provide more flexibility (1) as the sole trader can usually choose their own working hours and holidays etc. (1). **(2)**

2 **(c)** The workload and decision making can be shared. **(1)**

3 Any *two* from:

- Unlimited liability (1) – the partners are jointly responsible for all business debts and may have to sell their personal possessions (e.g. their home and car) to pay outstanding business debts (1). There is no limit on the amount that the partners can lose (1).
- There may be disagreement and conflict amongst partners (1) regarding business decisions and workload. This could delay decision making (1) and lead to problems running the business, especially if one partner pulls out of the business (1).
- It may take longer to reach business decisions (1) as all the partners need to be involved and consulted (1). There is a risk that the owners will be too slow making critical decisions which could result in competitors beating them to it and/or making problems worse (1).
- Profits must be shared amongst the partners (1). Each partner will only receive a share of the profit and that may not reflect the amount of work completed by each partner. If some partners contribute

more than others (1) this could cause resentment (1).

- Each partner is bound by the decisions that other partners make even (1) if they did not agree with them or were not aware of the decisions (1). This could cause problems if the decisions have serious implications (1). **(6)**

4 **(b)** A franchisee **(1)**

Page 95

1 **(a)** You are at risk of losing your personal possessions if the business goes into debt. **(1)**

2 **(b)** The owners must share the profit between them. **(1)**

3 Sole trader; partnership. **(2)**

4 Limited liability partnership; private limited company (Ltd). **(2)**

Page 96

1 **(b)** Grant **(1)**

2 **(a)** Capital provided by a bank with a formal repayment schedule that includes interest **(1)**

3 An experienced business owner who offers capital to support an entrepreneur to start or expand a business. They may ask for an equity stake in the business in return for the investment and/or a share of the profits earned. They may also ask to be involved in key decisions. **(2)**

4 **(a)** Any *two* from:

- Own savings
- Loans, e.g. a bank loan
- Crowdfunding
- Grants
- Business angels. **(2)**

(b) Any *one* advantage from:

- Generally do not have to pay interest, or if interest is paid on the capital it is often less than a bank would charge (1) which reduces expenses (1).

- No bank or lending fees (1) which reduces expenses (1).
- An informal agreement, so there is no formal contract (1) and it may be quicker to access the funds (1).
- Do not have to submit an application to borrow the money (1) so it may be quicker to access the funds (1).
- May be offered as a gift (1), and if so the capital will not have to be repaid (1).

Any *one* disadvantage from:

- As the arrangement is informal (1) it may lead to disagreements with family or friends (1).
- The friend or family member may interfere with decision making and/or the operations of the business (1) which may lead to a disagreement (1).
- Funds may have to be repaid at short notice if the friend or family member needs their money back (1), which will leave the entrepreneur short of funds (1).
- The entrepreneur may not be able to repay the money at short notice (1), which may lead to closure of the business (1).
- The amount of capital that is available may be limited (1), so the entrepreneur may need to use other sources of capital as well (1). **(4)**

Pages 97–98

1 **(b)** Accountant **(1)**

2 **(a)** Solicitor **(1)**

3 Any *two* from:
- Offer advice regarding the setting up/running of the business.
- Suggest sources of support for the entrepreneur, e.g. signpost the entrepreneur to others who can offer specific support.
- Act as a sounding board for ideas. The bank/business angel may ask to see a copy of a business plan from the entrepreneur and may be able to suggest ways of improving the business. **(2)**

4 Any *one* from:
- Financial support/source of capital (1). Charities often offer grants/loans for businesses that meet specific criteria, e.g. entrepreneurs of a specific age or someone looking to set up a business that will benefit the environment (1).
- Business advice (1). Many charities have dedicated advisers who can offer guidance for entrepreneurs (1).
- Training (1). Charities may offer specialist courses/events to develop the business skills of entrepreneurs or train them in a particular skill such as budgeting (1). **(2)**

5 Any *two* from:
- Joining a Chamber of Commerce will give Lyle the opportunity to meet other entrepreneurs in his local area (1). He will be able to network. Other entrepreneurs may be able to use Lyle's business (or recommend it to others) which will help his business gain more sales. Lyle may also be able to employ the services of other entrepreneurs that he meets at the Chamber of Commerce and they may offer him preferential prices/services (1).
- Chambers of Commerce may deliver training (1) which will enhance Lyle's business skills so he can run his business more effectively (1).
- Lyle will be able to attend regular meetings which will help him to keep up to date with developments and news (1) that will affect businesses in his local area. He will also find out about finance and business opportunities at the meetings (1).
- He will not be isolated as he will be able to share ideas (1) with the fellow entrepreneurs that he meets which can help him feel less isolated (1). **(4)**